THE NEW ECONOMICS

ONE DECADE OLDER

THE ELIOT JANEWAY LECTURES
ON HISTORICAL ECONOMICS
IN HONOR OF
JOSEPH SCHUMPETER
Princeton University
1972

THE NEW ECONOMICS

ONE DECADE OLDER

By James Tobin

PRINCETON UNIVERSITY PRESS

PRINCETON, NEW JERSEY

COPYRIGHT © 1974 BY PRINCETON UNIVERSITY PRESS
PUBLISHED BY PRINCETON UNIVERSITY PRESS,
PRINCETON AND LONDON

ALL RIGHTS RESERVED
LCC: 73-16763
ISBN: 0-691-04205-5

LIBRARY OF CONGRESS CATALOGING IN PUBLICATION DATA
WILL BE FOUND ON THE LAST PRINTED PAGE OF THIS BOOK

THIS BOOK HAS BEEN COMPOSED IN LINOTYPE TIMES ROMAN

PRINTED IN THE UNITED STATES OF AMERICA BY
PRINCETON UNIVERSITY PRESS,
PRINCETON, NEW JERSEY

Preface

In the spring of 1972 I was privileged to deliver the inaugural series of Janeway Lectures at the Woodrow Wilson School of Princeton University. I am very grateful to Dean Lewis and the faculty of the School for the invitation. It gave me the occasion to organize some reflections on macro-economic policy in the United States over the past dozen years.

Mr. Eliot Janeway, who honored the first lecture with his presence, had evidently expressed to the School his interest in lecturers who in some measure were inspired by Joseph A. Schumpeter. I do not know how well I met this preference, but I fully share Mr. Janeway's enthusiastic admiration of Schumpeter, who was my teacher, my dissertation adviser, and, in spite of many theoretical and political disagreements, my friend. I am afraid he would have been scornful of the "New Economics," but at least he would have endorsed its faith that the pragmatic mixture commonly called American capitalism was capable of sustained growth bringing increasing well-being to the masses of the population. And he would have been even more impatient than "New Economists" with the inhibitions on prosperity and progress proposed by monetarists and New Leftists. The development of a bourgeois intellectual New Left movement, incidentally, was foreseen with almost uncanny accuracy in Schumpeter's 1940 classic *Socialism, Capitalism and Democracy.*

Thanks to the Princeton University Press, I am publishing the three lectures here, essentially as they were prepared for delivery. I have made some editorial changes, and a few substantive ones. I have added some concluding remarks.

When Dean Lewis first intimated that I might be invited to give the lectures, he suggested that I might reflect on "The Keynesians, the Monetarists, the Treasury, and the 'Fed'." I took his suggestion, if not his title. I have always been fascinated by the connections between professional economic science and the terms of public discussion of economic issues, and by the intersection of these two influences in the actual making of economic policy in government.

The rise and fall—the fall, I think, is only partial and temporary—of the so-called New Economics in the sixties is an instructive chapter in the interaction of economics, public opinion, and government policy. The first chapter is devoted to that history, viewed from an admittedly biased perspective. The theme is continued in the second chapter, where I consider some currently fashionable attacks on the New Economics and the policies of the sixties associated with it, attacks from both the New Left and the monetarist Right. In the third chapter I try to draw from the experience of the last decade some lessons for economic stabilization policy in the future.

James Pugash, my undergraduate research aide at Yale, helped me prepare the lectures. Walter Heller came to the rescue of my memory on some points of history—

I have vastly larger debts to Walter not so specific to this volume. In revising the lectures for publication I have greatly benefited from Richard Lipsey's valuable and perceptive suggestions. It is a pleasure to acknowledge his help, since he was one of my hosts at the University of Essex in January 1966 when I delivered a Noel Buxton Lecture on "The Intellectual Revolution in U. S. Economic Policy-Making," covering some of the material reviewed here in Chapter 1. Finally, Sanford Thatcher of the Press has been a most helpful editor.

J.T.

CONTENTS

THE NEW ECONOMICS

ONE DECADE OLDER

1

Triumph and Defeat in the Sixties

Economics and Public Opinion, Then and Now

CAMELOT was scarcely ten years ago, but it has already evoked several decades' worth of poignant nostalgia, reminiscent chronicle, and revisionist history. The period since 1960 has been one of extraordinary changes, mostly unpredicted if not unpredictable, in the society, economy, and polity. National policies have changed, often drastically, and so have the frameworks of analysis and value in which issues of policy are formulated, debated, and decided.

In political economy, to return to Camelot is to revisit an era when growth was a good word, indeed *the* good word; when dollar devaluation was unthinkable; when automation was a hope and a scare; when poverty and inequality attracted little attention, and pollution even less; when protectionism was a sinful addiction requiring apology if not abstinence; when the Phillips curve had barely emerged from the economics journals; when a budget deficit was still a serious matter, and Eisenhower's $12.5 billion record was an upper bound; and when the quantity theory of money was a primitive doctrine mentioned in courses on the history of economic thought.

3

Like the economy itself, the stock of the American economics profession has gone up and down in the market of public opinion in the intervening years. It was low in 1960 and 1961. The tide of reaction against the New Deal on which Eisenhower swept into office in 1952 contained a wave of resentment and distrust of government and academic economists, especially strong in the business community. During the 1950s economists were demoted from policymaking roles in government—Arthur Burns[1] is a notable exception—and their views were rarely sought or heard in public discussion of economic issues.

The reversal in the 1960s was spectacular. Consider the transformation of Walter Heller[2] from an academician largely unknown in 1960 outside his profession and home town and accused, once Kennedy announced his appointment, of having offered typically impractical, unsound, New-Dealish advice to the new West German government right after the war. Now business leaders, labor groups, bankers' conventions, Congressional committees, and political candidates avidly seek his forecasts, diagnoses, and prescriptions.

[1] Director of Research of the National Bureau of Economic Research and Professor of Economics at Columbia in private life, Burns was Chairman of the Council of Economic Advisers to President Eisenhower, 1953-56. He returned to Washington in 1969 as a special Counsellor to President Nixon and in 1970 was appointed Chairman of the Board of Governors of the Federal Reserve System.

[2] Chairman of the Council of Economic Advisers 1961-64 under Presidents Kennedy and Johnson, Professor of Economics at the University of Minnesota in private life.

But Heller's continued personal prestige conceals a decline in the public appraisal of the profession at large. In the mid-sixties economists were riding the crest of a wave of enthusiasm and self-confidence. They seemed, after all, to have some tools of analysis and policy other people didn't have, and their policies seemed to be working. In the realm of macro-economics, at least, problems and issues were coming to be treated as technical rather than ideological. In his famous Yale Commencement speech in 1962, Kennedy had solicited a hostile audience to adopt, or at least tolerate, a pragmatic approach to economic policy in place of the emotions, slogans, myths, and shibboleths that had shaped business and financial attitudes ever since 1936. Two or three years later a Yale Commencement audience, even a Princeton alumni assembly, would have been much more receptive to the message.

From outside, the economics profession appeared quite unified, as befits a guild of technicians and pragmatists. Internal dissents there were, of course, but they made little public splash. The monetarists were gearing up for battle, but their manifestos hadn't yet appeared in *Newsweek*. Both old left and old right economists seemed to be voices of a past generation, as they were; new left and new right economists were not to emerge as powerful intellectual dissents until the turmoil of youth later in the decade. Even the ageless challenger of the conventional wisdom of his colleagues, J. K. Galbraith, was temporarily diverted in the first years of the decade by his own participation in government. The ecologists had not yet mounted attack on economists for allegedly wor-

5

shiping GNP without concern for the survival of the human race and other species.

Today, of course, things are very different. Economists have lost their short-lived reputation as pragmatic experts. Their disagreements are widely publicized, and so are their errors. The subject has become more ideological, and the profession has lost confidence in its own premises and methods. At recent meetings of the American Economic Association, the warmest applause has gone to speakers who told us how irrelevant and mistaken we are.

Major Ideas of the New Economics

The economics brought to Washington by the Kennedy Council of Economic Advisers[3] and other academic economists close to the new President was not new to economic literature and classrooms. It was not new in the practice of governments in Scandinavia, Holland, and Britain. Much of it was not new to official doctrine in this country, having been set forth by the first Councils of Economic Advisers, chaired by Edwin Nourse and Leon Keyserling for President Truman, and, in lesser degree, by the Eisenhower Councils as well.

But it was new to Washington nonetheless. The approach to economic policy was very different from the attitudes which the previous eight years had solidly entrenched in the Federal Reserve, and in the federal bu-

[3] The first Kennedy Council consisted of Walter Heller, Chairman, Kermit Gordon, and me. When I returned to Yale in August 1962, I was replaced by Gardner Ackley. But I maintained close consulting relations with the Council for several more years.

6

reaucracy, especially at the Treasury. It was new to the press—Washington reporters, financial writers, political commentators. They are the ones who coined the phrase "New Economics," innocent of economic theory and history and no doubt of the 1947 book on Keynesian economics edited by Seymour Harris.[4]

What were the major novelties of this New Economics? First was the conviction that business cycles were not inevitable, that government policy could and should keep the economy close to a path of steady real growth at a constant target rate of unemployment. At this date it may be difficult to recall how deeply ingrained the cycle was in 1960 in the economic thinking of practical men of government and business. At the time cyclical mentality was not an implausible inference from experience. Earlier history aside, the U. S. economy had by 1961 experienced four recessions since the end of the Second World War.

The cyclical mentality of practical men was reinforced by the dominant economists of the Eisenhower Administration, leaders or disciples of National Bureau business cycle research. The Mitchell–Burns–Moore tradition, after all, took an ever-repeating cycle for granted and sought to discover its empirical regularities. In 1960 business cycle chartism was at a peak, and much effort

[4] S. E. Harris, ed., *The New Economics* (New York: Knopf, 1947). The earliest use of the phrase with reference to Heller and the Kennedy Administration that my research assistant James Pugash can find is in *Newsweek*, July 16, 1962. The article entitled "Question: Is a Tax Cut What the Country Needs?" said: "Heller's brand of 'new economics,' with its emphasis on prediction and guidance of economic cycles, may be sweeping the Administration, but it has made no dent at all on Senator Byrd. . . ."

and attention were lavished on the classification of economic time series as leading, coincident, or lagging, and on the calculation of diffusion indexes and other derivative indicators.

Thanks to the interest of the Eisenhower Council, the Census Bureau prepared an increasingly elaborate monthly compilation of these statistics for circulation within the government. After the change of administrations, the question of continuing and indeed publishing such a compilation somehow fell into my lap. Some of my colleagues, particularly younger members of the Council staff, felt that the whole project was a good candidate for the new broom. But on the principle of letting many flowers bloom, I encouraged the publication of *Business Cycle Developments*, believing that many people in and out of government would find the compilation useful. Of course we insisted that the dating of cyclical turning points and the classifications of series as leading, coincident, or lagging be attributed to the National Bureau, not presented as official determinations of the government. The periodical has, I think, been a useful one, and the subsequent change of the meaning of its initials to *Business Conditions Digest* is itself an economic indicator.

In this climate of opinion, it was natural to think of government policy as partially compensatory, moderating swings but not preventing them. It was natural to think of upswings as having a powerful natural momentum, so that the task of government policy was not to sustain them but to restrain them. "Leaning against the wind" was the Fed's objective in the fifties. It was natural to think that the long-run track of the economy, around which cyclical

8

fluctuations occur, would take care of itself. It was natural to think that the upward drift in unemployment, measured by cyclical averages or peaks, must be a structural trend rather than something that policy had caused or could remedy.

Cyclical mentality was a major barrier to full employment policy. To counter it, the Kennedy Council introduced the concept of potential real GNP, estimated at a constant rate of utilization of productive resources, taken to be 4% unemployment. Potential GNP grows with labor force and productivity—at a rate first estimated as 3.5% but now raised to 4.3%. The percentage gap between actual and potential shows the loss of output due to underutilization. The rule of thumb known as Okun's Law[5] says that, for reasons familiar to all macro-economics students, one percentage point of unemployment translates into about three points of gap. Obviously the gap can be widening even while cyclical indicators are improving. Since the path of reference for judging economic performance is an ever-advancing target, it is small comfort to be told that economic indicators are gaining in absolute value. This is a lesson that is still incompletely learned, judging from Assistant Secretary of Commerce Harold Passer's weekly jubilation at any rise in any series and Council Chairman Herbert Stein's ill-tempered blast at Solomon Fabricant for suggesting that in 1971 the economy was still in a "growth recession."[6]

---

[5] Developed for the Council by Arthur M. Okun when he was a consultant commuting from Yale. He shortly became a senior staff member, later Member and Chairman.

[6] Stein told a fable in which Fabricant puzzled his friends by

9

Second, the New Economics sought to liberate federal fiscal policy from restrictive guidelines unrelated to the performance of the economy. The taboo on deficit spending, long discredited in the economics profession, had been reinforced by the White House during the Eisenhower years. Its strength both in influential circles and in general public opinion was a potent political force.

The full employment budget was a natural complement to the Council's emphasis on potential GNP. The concept was certainly far from novel, but it had not previously attracted much attention among noneconomists, even in the financial press. Today, of course, full employment budgeting has bipartisan blessing. For our Council it was a measuring device designed to distinguish deficits arising from weakness in the economy from those due to changes in federal expenditure programs and tax legislation. It was not a policy rule. The precept that the full employment budget should be balanced, adopted by the Nixon Administration, is another taboo for fiscal policy. It is, to be sure, less damaging than the ancient prescription of annual balance or the more modern one of balance over a cycle. But it is potentially confining—there are times when the full employment budget should be in deficit, 1972 for example, and other times when it should be in surplus.

With the help of the concepts of growing potential GNP and the full employment budget, the Kennedy

---

referring to his puppy as a "growth horse." Both the analogy and the humor escaped most people at the meeting at the National Bureau, of which Fabricant has long been a respected scholar.

Council sought to draw attention to long-run problems of fiscal policy. It is not enough that the federal budget be cyclically compensatory, leaning against the cyclical winds as revenues and outlays automatically respond to economic conditions. It is not even enough to reinforce these "built-in stabilizers" with discretionary counter-cyclical budget changes. It is also necessary that the secular level and trend of fiscal policy be consistent with the full employment growth track. It was Walter Heller, I believe, who coined the phrase "fiscal drag" to describe the secular tendency for fiscal policy to tighten—that is, for the full employment surplus to grow as a share of potential GNP—in the absence of deliberate decisions to increase real expenditures or reduce taxes. A related point emphasized by the Kennedy Council is that built-in stabilizers are not an unmixed blessing; they may stabilize the economy at too low a level.

Third, the 1961 Council sought to liberate monetary policy and to focus it squarely on the same macro-economic objectives that should guide fiscal policy. The attack on fiscal taboos caught the headlines. It was more dramatic, especially as it culminated in the 1964 tax cut. As a result, New Economists came to be identified as "fiscalists," a convenient antonym to "monetarists," later in the decade. But the fact is that Kennedy–Johnson economists believed strongly in the efficacy and importance of monetary policy. (Perhaps I should exclude J. K. Galbraith[7] from this consensus, as from some others.)

[7] Galbraith was an important and influential personal adviser to Kennedy before and after the 1960 election and during the

11

We adhered to the "neoclassical synthesis," which emphasized that monetary and fiscal ingredients could be mixed in varying proportions to achieve desired macroeconomic results. We did not subscribe to the Radcliffe Report[8] view, which relegated monetary policies and financial events to sideshow status.

From what did monetary policies need to be liberated in 1961? There were plenty of taboos against the aggressive use of monetary expansion to restore full employment. One was "bills only," a Wall Street doctrine that arrived in Washington in 1953. According to "bills only" doctrine, open market operations should virtually always be conducted in Treasury bills.

Perhaps even more important was the Fed's allergy, stemming from the days before the Accord of 1951,[9] to any market interventions that smacked of rate-pegging or rate-setting, even for short periods of time. In general, the Fed attached unreasonably high priority to the maintenance of healthy conditions in the securities markets— not sloppy, not thin—to protection of the quality of credit, and to the avoidance of unsound speculation. The leaders of the Fed believed that they had just won a hard battle against the inflationary psychology of the mid-fifties, a

---

early days of the Administration. Even after he went to India as Ambassador, he continued to offer the President advice on economic matters, especially during his periodic visits to Washington. See his *Ambassador's Journal: A Personal Account of the Kennedy Years* (Boston: Houghton Mifflin, 1969).

[8] Committee on the Working of the Monetary System, Report Cmnd. 827 (London: HMSO, 1959).

[9] The Accord released the Federal Reserve from its wartime commitment to support the price of Treasury securities, an undertaking which had rendered the Fed powerless to oppose postwar inflation.

12

triumph they were not anxious to throw away in hope of reducing unemployment. Anyway, according to Federal Reserve Chairman William McChesney Martin, the rise in unemployment was mainly a structural malady for which demand stimulus was the wrong medicine.

At that time economic analysis was not as important an ingredient of Federal Reserve policymaking as it later became. In 1961 the Board of Governors included no professional economists among its seven members; at the beginning of 1972 there were five, though one was on the way out. In 1961 the research staff contained some excellent people but did not have the professional stature it had enjoyed ten to fifteen years earlier and was to regain five to ten years later.

Added to the host of chimerical and self-imposed inhibitions on monetary policy was one major external constraint, the balance of payments. Short-term interest rates could not be pushed or held too low without driving funds out of the country.

Fourth, the New Economics was growth-oriented. In this respect it was in tune with popular and political opinion, at least semantically. The United States was widely believed to be stagnating while other economies, east and west of the Iron Curtain, were inexorably accelerating. Getting the country moving again was part of 1960 campaign rhetoric, and a speech against growthmanship that some Republican economist wrote for Nixon was one of the losing candidate's least successful ploys. Not long after the 1961 inauguration, believe it or not, all offices and desks in the Commerce Department sported placards asking "What have you done for Growth today?"

The New Economics carefully distinguished between

13

growth of potential, a matter of supply and productive capacity, and recovery of actual output to potential levels, a matter of aggregate demand. True to the neoclassical synthesis, we pointed out that some ways of restoring full employment are more favorable to growth of capacity than others. Growth would be fostered by mixtures of policy that would leave plenty of room in a full employment economy for accumulation of public and private capital and at the same time would stimulate enough investment demand to fill the space. Easy monetary policy and the investment tax credit were part of such a package, and policies to raise permanently the national propensity to consume were not. This is why I, at least, was reluctant to opt for permanent reduction of the income tax until I was convinced that other ways of expanding demand were economically or politically blocked.

But a really aggressive monetary expansion was not in the cards because of the balance of payments. And temporary reduction of the income tax could not be sold politically. A tax cut had to be billed as a structural reform, releasing the energy and enterprise of the American people from oppressive tax rates left over from the Korean war. The notion that its purpose was to release money to be spent, at a time when the economy was already on an upswing, was not quite respectable. To be very specific, it was not respectable with Congressman Wilbur Mills.[10]

[10] Chairman of the Ways and Means Committee of the House of Representatives, then as now the most powerful member of Congress with respect to tax and fiscal policy.

14

Of course the distinction between long-run growth of capacity and short-run growth of aggregate demand was a fairly sophisticated point, and it was never, I fear, very effectively or persuasively communicated. Among other things, it precipitated a conflict with Democratic and trade union economists of an older generation and tradition, notably Leon Keyserling. They were underconsumptionists to whom growth policy meant, and still means, undifferentiated government spending, plus transfer programs and wage increases to raise consumption demand by wage earners and other households of high marginal propensity to spend. They did not believe that investment could be stimulated except by raising consumption demand.

Fifth, the New Economics established a specific full employment goal, defined for an open-ended interim as 4% unemployment. Why 4%? Young Turks on the Council staff thought the figure was too high, an unholy compromise of the principles of the Employment Act with political practicalities. Willard Wirtz, then Undersecretary of Labor, thought it disgustingly inhumane to suggest that the Administration would settle for any unemployment at all. Of course we were talking about a target for aggregate demand policy, for monetary and fiscal measures, and we assigned to the structural labor market policies dear to Wirtz's heart the task of lowering the target below 4%.

The more dangerous flak was coming from the other direction, from those who said that demographic and technological changes had increased the incidence of mismatches between jobs and workers. In those days almost

15

everyone outside the economics profession, and a few inside it, thought that automation was rapidly eliminating jobs, that all but the most technically educated were becoming unemployable, that the pace of technical progress was going to produce one Appalachia after another. Such diverse people as William McChesney Martin, Robert Theobald,[11] and Congressman Thomas Curtis (the acknowledged Republican economic pundit of the Congress and the Joint Economic Committee) agreed on the general lines of the diagnosis. They didn't agree on what the remedy was, but they all knew what it was not—namely, expansion of aggregate demand.

One of the first tasks we set ourselves at the Council was to refute this diagnosis. Our refutation, to which staff members Robert Solow and Edward Kalachek contributed mightily, was gloriously confirmed by the ease with which new jobs were created and unemployment diminished in the subsequent expansion of aggregate demand. However, there is now some evidence that the demographic portion of the structuralist case began to come true in the last half of the decade, about ten years late.[12]

Four percent was chosen with an eye on the Phillips

[11] Popular author of *Free Men and Free Markets* (New York: Clarkson N. Potter, 1963) and other books and articles arguing that because automation was making human labor obsolete a radically new economic system divorcing income from productive employment was imperative.

[12] George Perry, "Changing Labor Markets and Inflation," *Brookings Papers on Economic Activity*, 1970, No. 3, pp. 466-73. Charles Schultze, "Has the Phillips Curve Shifted? Some Additional Evidence," *Brookings Papers on Economic Activity*, 1971, No. 2, pp. 452-68.

curve, specifically on the 4% inflation that accompanied 4% unemployment in the mid-1950s. We could not be sure whether this was indicative of what 4% unemployment would bring in the future. We could be sure that a more ambitious employment target would be considered irresponsibly inflationary by many influential critics at home and abroad. Their opposition might cripple an expansionary policy. The view that U.S. balance-of-payments deficits were the natural divine retribution for inflationary fiscal and monetary policies—punishment from which not even the U.S. could expect to be exempt —had been espoused by no less an authority than the prestigious Managing Director of the International Monetary Fund, Per Jacobsson, and had a numerous following in New York as well as Zurich. They were talking about Eisenhower policies!

Commitment to a lower figure than 4% seemed a battle scarcely worth joining in 1961. With unemployment then at almost 7%, with 4% a four-year-old memory, it seemed more urgent to start moving in the right direction than to settle in advance how far to go. For the same reasons we gave high priority to measures to minimize the inflationary content of the recovery. The principal measures, apart from manpower programs and regional development efforts, were the wage-price guideposts.

Finally, the Kennedy Council was very much afraid that the international position of the dollar would be a serious obstacle to policies for domestic expansion and growth. At the same time we did not regard balance-of-payments deficits as a reason to restrict international

17

movements of goods and capital or to curtail intrinsically useful government programs overseas. On these points the conflict within the government was not so much new economics against old as economics against established attitudes and institutions. In our view, risks could be taken, for if worst came to worst and the dollar had to be rendered inconvertible into gold and depreciated against other currencies, that worst would be an innocuous and even favorable outcome. We believed the U.S. should push for reform of the Bretton Woods gold-dollar system because the U.S. had little further to gain from perpetuating it. By 1972 these were scarcely breathtaking positions, but ten years before they were regarded as dangerous heresies. I shall return to this battle later in this chapter.

The Constraints and Their Relaxation: Domestic Policy

The New Economics did not come to Washington as the agreed doctrine of the new Administration, much less of its fellow Democrats in Congress or of the numerous constituencies whose support or acquiescence the Administration regarded as necessary. In fact, the New Economics began with virtually no adherents outside the Executive Office Building, home of the Council and its natural ally, the Budget Bureau. The Council's problem was educational rather than analytical. From a technical standpoint, diagnosis and prescription were easy in 1961. Expansionary policy was clearly the indicated medicine, and there was no practical possibility of an overdose.

18

Forecasting accuracy was not terribly important, except in relation to the Council's credibility. There was little economic danger that an underforecast would lead to excessive governmental stimulus, and little prospect that overoptimism would lead to too little stimulus. The problem was to persuade the White House, the Executive, the Congress, the Federal Reserve, and the public of the obvious point that the economy needed more aggregate demand.

President Kennedy came to office without any firm understanding or conviction in macro-economic matters. Campaign rhetoric had developed no clear line. He had received, but not absorbed, conflicting advice from various economists: Harris and Galbraith, Samuelson and Tobin, Keyserling and other old-line Democratic economists. His father had evidently pressed on him strong and mostly conservative views on economic matters. His campaign had taken a conservative stance on fiscal policy. But he had made some populist speeches—Galbraithian in origin, I believe—expressing views on monetary policy that scared the financial communities of New York and Europe. He had been elected by a narrow margin without a popular majority. His party had uncomfortably small majorities in Congress and was dominated by senior conservatives, mostly from the South, who felt no particular loyalty or political obligation to him. He and his principal adviser Theodore Sorenson decided early on that the New Frontier must consolidate its domestic political base before embarking on bold new initiatives in domestic policy in general and economic policy in particular.

19

General unemployment per se was not seen as a politically important issue, nor were great political benefits perceived from reducing it by diffuse and indirect macroeconomic measures whose connection with jobs is a mystery to the electorate and even to the newly employed. Chronic unemployment in West Virginia, and direct federal help to relieve it—there a politician can see the problem and hope to reap credit for a remedy. Ted Sorenson asked me why I was so anxious to cut unemployment a few percentage points; the difference between employment rates of 93% and 96% seemed to him like the difference between grades of A— and A, hardly an improvement on which to expend political capital. He eventually was persuaded that moving from 93% to 96% alters lots of other important variables very significantly.

Recessions of course are politically dangerous, as Republican defeats in 1932, 1954, 1958, 1960—we might add 1970—indicate. But a first-derivative mentality is strong in American politics. Provided economic indicators are moving up, their level is secondary. Incidentally, politico-econometric studies of the influence of economic variables on elections confirm this instinctive feeling of politicians: the current growth rate of GNP counts for votes, but not the level of unemployment.[13] Not surprisingly, economists advocating stimulative policy get a better hearing in the White House and Congress and the Federal Reserve when they can point to actual or impending recession than when they simply want to boost an ongoing expansion.

[13] Gerald H. Kramer, "Short-term Fluctuations in U.S. Voting Behavior," *The American Political Science Review*, LXV, March 1971, 131-43.

The caution of the new Administration became evident even before inauguration. Kennedy had great respect for experts, including thinkers from academic ivory towers. He liked to have their proposals before him even if they turned out to be politically impracticable for the time being. He assembled a number of pre-inauguration task forces to make policy recommendations. A task force on the domestic economy was chaired by Paul Samuelson, and one on foreign economic policy by George Ball. But meanwhile he had appointed Douglas Dillon as Secretary of the Treasury and Robert Roosa as Undersecretary. Alarmed by the prospect that the Samuelson and Ball task forces might set unsound lines of policy for the new Administration, and in the Treasury's domain at that, Dillon and Roosa prevailed upon the President-elect to establish as a counterweight another task force on economic policy, chaired by Allen Sproul, retired President of the Federal Reserve Bank of New York.[14] The Sproul report set the lines of balance of payments policy and emphasized the constraints on domestic expansion. Although the Sproul and Samuelson reports were published, the Ball report was not.

More important, Sorenson informed the Samuelson

[14] Other members of the Sproul Committee were Professor Roy Blough of Columbia, a Member of the Council under Truman, and Professor Paul McCracken of the University of Michigan, a Member under Eisenhower and later Chairman under Nixon. The Committee's hue of conservative respectability matched that of the new Treasury leadership. Dillon, an investment banker, was the outgoing Republican Undersecretary of State, and Roosa was Vice President of the Federal Reserve Bank of New York.

task force in the course of its deliberations that the political elbow room for expansionary budget policy was very small. The new Administration felt boxed in by the fiscal 1962 budget submitted by President Eisenhower. A budget deficit could be tolerated only to the extent it could be blamed on erroneous estimates of revenues and outlays by the outgoing Administration. The prevailing political view was that public acceptance of the Administration was too precarious, especially in the business and financial community at home and abroad, and the vulnerability of Democrats to charges of unsound fiscal and financial practice was too great, to allow a more adventurous policy.

Congress is in the last analysis the maker of budget policy, and macro-economic considerations naturally take a back seat in its deliberations. In the early sixties even economically literate liberals in the Senate and House would not go out on a limb for expansionary fiscal policy. Liberal members of Congress were natural monetarists, and indeed they still are. If the Fed can be blamed for the general state of the economy, there is nothing that Congress can or need do. Take, for example, Senator William Proxmire, a man I greatly admire. As a freshman Senator, he had been badly burned in Wisconsin when President Eisenhower attacked him for irresponsibly espousing a pile of expensive liberal programs. His reaction to our pleas for fiscal expansion in 1961-62 was that there was nothing wrong with the economy that Bill Martin couldn't fix if he only would. I was not surprised some years later when the Joint Economic Committee under his leadership endorsed a Friedmanite rule for Federal Reserve policy.

The monetarist proclivities of Congress work in both directions. If inflation is the fault of the Fed, why bother Congress for tax increases? But there are more important and obvious reasons why Congress neglects macro-economic considerations in tax and budget legislation. Issues of distributive equity, the specific interests of taxpayers and beneficiaries of proposed expenditures, are bound to be in the forefront.

Gradually, but only gradually, the political constraints relaxed. Within them we were able to contrive some fiscal stimulus by various devices that preserved the cosmetics of the administrative budget, raising social security benefits in advance of the inevitably associated increases in payroll taxes, selling government loans to private lenders, accelerating tax collections and rearranging the timing of government outlays. One appeal of the investment tax credit, apart from its other advantages, was the prospect of considerable economic bang per budgetary buck.

A major victory was the decision in the summer of 1961 not to match the Berlin buildup of defense expenditures with increased taxes. Everyone else in the Administration favored the taxes, and only vehement protests from the Council, seconded by Samuelson, saved the day at the last minute. Even then the President felt he must excuse the resulting deficit by a pledge that his fiscal 1963 budget, to be submitted in January 1962, would be balanced. This hostage to fiscal respectability was a real

23

constraint, even though the revenue estimates in the submitted budget were thought by many critics—and in the event correctly—to be based on an overoptimistic economic forecast for 1962.

During 1962 the President changed tack, for several reasons. The recovery was faltering, and it became clear that he could not realistically produce balanced budgets. He was not even getting points for trying; business antagonism to the Administration had, if anything, accentuated, partly in delayed reaction to the steel price confrontation of April 1962. Meanwhile he had become intellectually convinced of the Council's case. Innocent of economics on inauguration day, he was an interested and an apt pupil of the professors in the Executive Office Building. He was impressed that the Council had so far been right in predicting, contrary to other advisers, that with unemployed men and excess capacity expansion could and would proceed without price inflation.

In the summer of 1962 he was on the verge of recommending tax reduction to pep up the expansion. There were some signs that the time was ripe. The U.S. Chamber of Commerce had issued a statement in favor of tax cuts, although it was ambiguous on the question whether they should be coupled with matching cuts in expenditure. A trial balloon was launched. But it was shot down. Soundings indicated that an unmatched tax cut would not be immune from attacks from the business and financial establishment. The Treasury was not ready. Secretary Dillon argued that an emergency demand-stimulating tax cut would be regarded as unsound in New York and Europe, while a deliberately prepared tax cut incident to the structural tax reform his department was in the process of designing would be understood and applauded. Moreover, tax reduction must be saved to lubricate tax reform. Wilbur Mills agreed with the Treasury. The President announced that legislation for tax reduction and reform would be introduced in January 1963.

The President did not live to see the ultimate result, the Revenue Act of 1964. The delay was risky. Monetary policy, the investment tax credit, modest budgetary expansion on the expenditure side, the momentum of the private economy, and sheer luck kept the expansion going in the interim. And as the Council had predicted, the delay did not save the Treasury's tax reforms. The Congress showed itself quite capable of stripping reforms from the bill.

Galbraith, Keyserling, and others have criticized the Council for recommending tax reduction rather than increases of civilian expenditure to meet social needs. The Council agreed with their sense of priorities; the public sector was undernourished. The Council consistently pushed the expenditure side of the budget. But the political limits to deficit spending in that guise were even more stringent than the obstacles to tax reduction. The effective alternative was not a larger expenditure budget but continuing fiscal drag, with every prospect that the recovery, like the previous upswing in 1960, would be aborted short of full employment.

Other critics have also pointed out, with the benefit of hindsight, that the economy would have been better off in 1966 with unreduced taxes. That is true, but the escalation in Vietnam was scarcely foreseeable three or

25

four years in advance. Moreover, this criticism is not consistent with the Galbraith–Keyserling complaint. If civilian expenditures had been increased by the $12 billion by which taxes were reduced, the fiscal outcome would have been no less inflationary in 1966. It would have been no less necessary to face the painful choice among allowing unchecked inflation, raising taxes, and curbing civilian expenditures. In the event it was politically very difficult to reverse the previous tax reductions. It would have been even more painful, politically and substantively, to make drastic cutbacks in recently expanded expenditure programs.

Nevertheless, with the added hindsight available in 1972, I must admit there is truth in the claim that the 1964 tax cut set a bad precedent. The 1964 example may have contributed to the tax reductions of 1971; at any rate, it certainly muted or discredited some of the natural opposition to those proposals from Democratic economists and politicians. The situation was superficially similar, a stagnant economy in need of fiscal stimulus. If a permanent loss of federal revenue was the right policy in 1964, why not in 1971?

The subtle answer is that events have, for the time being anyway, more than overcome the fiscal drag that concerned Walter Heller ten or twelve years ago. The list of federal expenditure programs on the agenda of both parties is long and expensive: welfare reform, revenue sharing, day care, education, environment, mass transit, defense. There is no longer a danger that the full employment budget surplus will automatically and unmanageably grow in the absence of periodic tax reduction.[15] On the contrary, the danger is that unless the federal revenue base is restored, either the needed expenditure programs will be postponed or sacrificed, or their inflationary impact will have to be offset by very restrictive monetary policy. If permanent tax cuts are enacted whenever the economy needs cyclical stimulus—as well as at other times, as in 1969—and monetary restriction is invoked whenever deflationary medicine is called for, there is a secular ratchet effect toward a fiscal-monetary mix unfavorable to capital accumulation. It is true that this trend is mitigated to the extent that the tax reductions, like the tax credit reenacted in 1971, are inducements to investments rather than consumption. But going any further down that road, or even as far as we have gone, is objectionable on grounds of distributive equity, and probably efficiency too. What we needed in 1971, and very likely in 1964 as well, were temporary tax reductions, expiring automatically after eighteen months or two years.

Constraints and Their Relaxation: International Monetary Policy

The same timidity that characterized the Kennedy Administration's initial approach to domestic economic policy pervaded its approach to the international dollar crisis inherited from its predecessor. I have already referred to the pre-inauguration efforts of the new Treasury

[15] See the series of books by Charles Schultze et al., *Setting National Priorities* (Washington, D.C.: Brookings Institution, 1970, 1971, 1972).

27

leadership to head off the radical proposals they suspected the Ball task force might produce. An immediate issue in January 1961 was whether the Administration should ask for reduction or repeal of the "gold cover" reserve requirements against Federal Reserve notes and deposit liabilities. The new Treasury leadership actually favored some such move, to make clear that the gold was free to meet our international convertibility commitments. The idea was scotched by Galbraith and Sorenson, who feared domestic political repercussions if the first act of a new Democratic Administration, like that of Roosevelt in 1933, could be said to be "tinkering with the money." The incident was more symptomatic than substantive; eventually the obsolete gold reserve requirements were removed in stages with no trouble. But it does indicate how vulnerable the Kennedy Administration felt to potential charges that through irresponsibility or inexpertise it mishandled the balance of payments.

President Kennedy took an active and anxious personal interest in the problem, and for a long time he viewed it from a very simplistic and physical model of payments deficits. More money goes out of the country than comes in, and money is gold. The remedy seemed simple too: stop the money from going out, especially when the government itself is sending it overseas. That is why the Budget Bureau was directed to assemble from Departments a so-called "gold budget" of overseas expenditures. His fears were reinforced both by the Treasury, whose overriding objective was to maintain gold convertibility of an undervalued dollar, and by advisers

28

like Galbraith, who saw the weakness of the dollar as undermining the Administration's diplomatic strength abroad and political strength at home.

Education of the President went more slowly on international trade and finance than on domestic macro-economics. I recall an excited phone call from the President one Saturday afternoon asking me, in Heller's absence, to have the Council mount a new effort to slash the "gold budget." I agreed we would start collecting the needed information but said I thought it was very much the wrong approach. He was shocked but listened attentively to my explanation, and invited a memo and a discussion in the Oval Office. There were many such memos and discussions, before and after. A breakthrough occurred when Kermit Gordon and I managed to apprise the President of the fact that no gold left the country without a deliberate political decision by a foreign government—France under President de Gaulle, for a notable example—to ask for conversion of dollars. Once he understood that, he could see our point that the dollar problem was an international one, subject to political negotiation, not just the fault and responsibility of the United States. By 1963 I knew from personal conversation and from participation in White House meetings on the subject that the President was intellectually convinced the U.S. could and should accept some risks that the dollar might some day have to become inconvertible and float. He saw that some measures advocated to "save" the dollar—for example, limits on U.S. tourism—were worse than not saving it.

29

In international monetary affairs the Treasury has the operating responsibility and the power, and it is difficult for anyone else in the Executive branch, or in Congress for that matter, to have any influence. The Council tried, with the help of the economists on the White House National Security staff, Carl Kaysen and later Francis Bator. Our efforts yielded both frustration and friction, although personal relations with the Treasury were always friendly.[16]

The State Department was a natural ally of the Council, but a hopelessly ineffectual one. State might be expected to resist balance of payments measures that place restrictions on trade, capital movements, foreign aid, and foreign policy, and to favor international monetary reform. State might be expected, on purely bureaucratic grounds, to resist wholesale surrender to the Treasury of so central an aspect of foreign economic policy. These were indeed Undersecretary Ball's inclinations, but when the chips were down, he and his Department were unwilling to expend for this cause any of their credit in the White House or the Cabinet. The same was true of the top leaders of the Department of Defense. They were more afraid of the risk that defense appropriations would suffer if the Pentagon were blamed for the balance of pay-

[16] One of our greatest sins in 1961, it turned out, was to use Yale Professor Robert Triffin as a consultant; Triffin's early warnings and proposals, beginning in 1957, on the international monetary system are now acknowledged to have been prophetic, but in those days he was regarded in the Treasury as a dangerous radical. See Robert Triffin, *Gold and the Dollar Crisis* (New Haven: Yale University Press, 1960).

ments deficit than of the costs and inconveniences imposed upon their overseas procurement and personnel by "gold budget" economies.

Robert Roosa ran the show, with Secretary Dillon's complete and capable support. Roosa is a man of tremendous ability, intelligence, energy, and self-confidence. His mission, as he saw it, was to save the gold-convertible dollar at its existing parity and to preserve the dollar's reserve currency status. The threats, as he saw them, were both external—the chronic balance of payments deficit and the pressures of our European creditors—and internal—the pressures for international monetary reform from those of us in the government who gave his objectives lower priority than other goals of domestic and foreign policy. In his view, even the slightest hints of American open-mindedness to change would destroy foreign confidence and precipitate runs on gold. In those days even to mention the possibility of gold or exchange value guarantees of outstanding balances was taboo, and infinitely more so any admission of the eventual possibilities of exchange rate adjustments, internationally created reserves, or changes in the status of gold.

At the same time Roosa carried out a masterful strategy of expedient retreat, designed to shore up the existing system without altering its essential features. His expedients included swap agreements between the Federal Reserve and other central banks, providing mutual credit lines with exchange guarantees; exchange-guaranteed Treasury bills and other devices to make dollar holdings more attractive and remunerative for foreign central

31

banks; advance repayments of European long-term debts to the United States; an agreement by which European countries would lend to the IMF to increase the availability of their currencies for drawings by others (opposed by the Council to the extent that it gave the Common Market countries a veto over drawings to which the U.S. was entitled by right). Note that many of these measures embodied features that Roosa had initially found unacceptable.

Meanwhile the U.S. reacted to periodic crises by successively tightening the screws on governmental and private outlays abroad: tying foreign aid to purchases in the U.S., "buy American" preferences in government procurement; reducing duty-free tourist imports; levying the interest equalization tax; imposing controls, compulsory or semi-voluntary, on bank lending overseas and corporate direct investment.

Roosa agreed with us in forcing Operation Twist, with its abandonment of "bills only," on the Fed. The objective was to raise short-term rates relative to long rates, on the theory that short rates were the more important for international movements of funds and the long rates for domestic investment and residential construction. There probably wasn't much in it, but it was never really tried. For one thing, the Fed really didn't like to buy in the long-term market and would never do so if its purchases might change market prices. More important, Roosa himself was also in charge of debt management and saw his mission there to be lengthening the average maturity of the debt, which he did with the help of numerous advance refundings. In vain I remonstrated

32

that, in terms of the relative supplies of short and long securities in public hands, the Treasury was more than undoing the Fed's timid operations.

Roosa's fingers plugged the dike for several years, but his holding strategy delayed any far-reaching international resolution or even discussion of the basic problems, an evasion which made the Europeans increasingly restless. It was not until Secretary Henry H. Fowler took over in 1965 and made international monetary reform a personal objective that the whole subject was opened up. The unthinkable began to be thinkable and even sayable, and many ideas previously suppressed or sidetracked came into their own, such as the creation of new reserves—paper gold, SDR's—by international agreement in the IMF. A big step toward demonetization of gold was taken by the 1968 agreement of governments to stay out of private gold markets. The need for exchange rate adjustments, and the merits of alternative systems of bringing them about, emerged from academic into official discussion. Secretary Fowler even intimated that, in the absence of cooperation from the surplus countries, worse things could happen to the U.S. than an inconvertible floating dollar. Of course the final irony[17] is that this outcome, which a Democratic Administration suffered such pain to avoid in fear of adverse political reaction from the right, was engineered into a triumph of statesmanship by a Republican Administra-

---

[17] An irony, but a common one. Harold Wilson's Labor government defended an unrealistic sterling parity long after pragmatic Tories would have given up. A noneconomic example: it was a Republican President who made friends with China.

33

tion. It is true, but probably not significant, that both Kennedy and Nixon had Secretaries of the Treasury of opposite political party.

Vietnam, Inflation, and Disillusionment

Through 1965 the management of the domestic economy under the New Economics was a great success, and was generally perceived as such. The economy had enjoyed uninterrupted expansion for five years. The 4% unemployment target had virtually been attained. Real GNP had grown by 31%, and 6.8 million new jobs had been created. Prices were rising at the moderate and tolerable rate of 2% per year. The great tax cut had apparently worked as advertised. Within the Administration New Economics had become official orthodoxy, and Walter Heller and his successors the acknowledged master architects of economic policy. The Treasury had long since climbed on the bandwagon. Even the Federal Reserve Board, its membership changed, had been cooperative, though their independent hike of the discount rate in December and Martin's outburst on the "lessons of 1929" showed they were more apprehensive of the future than the Administration was. Then things began to fall apart.

Evidently the Pentagon did not tell the Council, Budget Bureau, and Treasury how rapidly it was letting contracts in 1965 and spending money in 1966. Evidently the Council nevertheless advised President Johnson to recommend a tax increase in the January 1966 budget and economic messages, and the advice was re-

34

jected. Evidently the President feared that Congress would not enact such a proposal but seize the admission of the need for a tighter budget as an excuse for cutting back expenditures on his Great Society programs. In this political judgment he was probably right. When belatedly he did propose a tax increase, he obtained it only after a bizarre treaty with Wilbur Mills, which exacted of the President budget economies below Congressional appropriations.

Meanwhile the burden of restraint fell almost wholly on the Fed, which acted vigorously and courageously. Its tightening was too late, perhaps, but could hardly be said to be too little. The power of monetary restraint was dramatically and convincingly demonstrated. But so too was its uneven impact: residential construction was suddenly cut 25%, while business investment remained unscathed until later. The Fed no doubt tested the outer limits of public tolerance of sudden monetary restriction.

After the 1966 credit crunch, it seems to me, the Administration and the Fed scrambled about as skillfully as Yale quarterback Brian Dowling eluding Princeton pursuers. With the help of good forecasting, appropriate measures were taken, or at least proposed, well in advance of the economic conditions that motivated them. The restoration in the spring of 1967 of the investment tax credit, suspended the previous October, is a fine example of flexible fiscal policy. Anticipatory fine-tuning prevented the checking of the 1966 boom from developing into a full-fledged inventory recession in 1967, a sequence that almost surely would have occurred ten or twenty years before.

35

During the 1967 hesitation the Council correctly fore-saw the renewed expansion ahead, and the President finally asked for an income tax surcharge. But Congress could not see the need for it and did not act until June 1968 when a strong expansion was already well under way. The effects of the surcharge, once finally enacted, were disappointing—a matter which I shall discuss later —and so the Johnson Administration bequeathed its successors an overheated economy along with its program of gradual disinflation. Neither the bequeathers nor the heirs, nor outside observers either, realized then how stubbornly persistent the wage-price inflation ignited by the overheating would prove to be.

The validity of New Economics as science is, of course, not impaired but rather reinforced by the fact that bad things happened as predicted when the advice of its practitioners was rejected. The economic efficacy of fiscal policy is confirmed, not refuted, by the powerful stimulus that Vietnam deficit spending delivered to the economy.

Of course the public had no way to know the true views of the Council in 1966 because as loyal advisers to the President they could not express them publicly. Some may feel that the issue was so central, failure to act so damaging to the future of economic policy under the Employment Act, that Council members should have resigned. But this is hindsight, no doubt colored by the subsequent unpopularity of the Vietnam war, and it is impossible for us as outsiders to imagine all the considerations and pressures involved.

The episode demonstrated that the New Economics had been oversold, probably less by its practitioners than by interpreters in the press. I don't know who first used the term "fine-tuning," but its wide currency stuck the New Economics with the image of Walter Heller constantly and precisely adjusting dials to keep the economy on track. Never mind that he and his successors harbored no such illusion. In 1966 and subsequently it became painfully clear that economists do not have enough tools of foresight, analysis, and policy to enable the government to avoid or offset shocks to the economy. Of course the Vietnam escalation was one hell of a shock; severe tests of that order will not be very frequent. Nevertheless the experience brought home several deficiencies in the arsenal of stabilization policy. Compensating fiscal measures are generally very slow, and just because sensitive questions of equities and priorities are involved, political considerations take precedence over stabilization objectives. Monetary policy is more flexible and mobile, and less distracted by considerations extraneous to economic stabilization. But, given the U.S. financial structure, sudden large doses of monetary tightness are painful and inequitable. I shall return to these issues in the third chapter.

The inflationary consequences of low unemployment were an even more serious blow to the reputation of the New Economics. The public had come to expect too much and felt let down. Somehow the impression had been conveyed that the New Economics promised full employment, steady growth, and price stability too. The facts of life pictured in the Phillips curve came as a shock.

Had we economists failed to come clean? Perhaps, although the steepness of the Phillips curve below 4%

37

unemployment was an unpleasant surprise to us as well. The 1962 Economic Report, in the course of explaining the 4% unemployment target, contains an extended discussion of the Phillips problem. But little public attention was paid to such remote contingencies in those days. No President, Presidential candidate, or other political leader of either party has ever cared or dared to admit to the electorate that full employment and price stability are incompatible goals. Official messages and campaign speeches are full of the fallacy that will makes way: since it is unthinkable that the objectives cannot be simultaneously met, there simply must be a way to reconcile them. Like other approaches to economic policy, the New Economics was popularly advertised as the road to salvation in every dimension. When the Phillips trade-off problem became acute, as very probably would have happened in some degree even without Vietnam, the unprepared public became disillusioned with stabilization policy in general.

Another serious consequence of the failure to educate the country on the inflationary bias of the economy has been, in my view, a vast exaggeration of the social costs of inflation. Presidential and political rhetoric ritualistically condemns inflation as an unbearable evil, and economists in public life, New Economists as well as others, have generally acquiesced in this stance. We know in our hearts that the trend of prices in this country, and in the world at large, has been and will be inexorably upward. Yet the standard view throughout the society is that this trend can be halted, indeed must be halted to avert catastrophe. Maybe it would be healthy for the country

38

TRIUMPH AND DEFEAT IN THE SIXTIES

to have an explicit public debate about which point on the Phillips trade-off we should aim for. There undoubtedly is a real difference between the parties in the values they attach to low unemployment and price stability. But the difference is suppressed by the insistence of both sides that they know how to achieve both goals at once.

2

Crossfire from Left and Right

In this second chapter I propose to consider some contemporary attacks on the New Economics of the 1960s and on the associated economic policies of that decade. Some come from the left, some from the right; some are hard to place in political spectrum. I shall begin with those that come primarily from the left, and among them with charges relating to the economic role of defense and war.

The New Economics and War Spending

Marxists have argued for generations that war is an intrinsic economic consequence of capitalism; the youthful New Left, including the growing band of radical economists, have rediscovered and reasserted this proposition.

In the hands of Baran and Sweezy[1] and other economically literate radicals, the proposition takes a sophisticated form. Technological progress in the productivity of labor and capital creates an ever-widening gap between full employment saving and profitable investment. Employment high enough to prevent dangerous disaffection

[1] Paul Baran and Paul Sweezy, *Monopoly Capital* (New York: Monthly Review Press, 1966).

41

from the system can be preserved only by filling the gap with unproductive expenditure. Most of this must be government expenditure, and the only large politically acceptable public expenditures are for defense and war. Civilian spending is an unacceptable outlet. Substantive projects, like public housing, compete with private enterprise, and transfer programs, like welfare, undermine the supply of disciplined low-wage labor.

The events of the sixties lend superficial credence to the position. It can be said, it is said, that full employment was not achieved until the escalation of the Vietnam War. The Marxists and New Leftists have an unlikely ally in President Nixon, who has repeatedly said that the U.S. has in the past not achieved full employment in peacetime.[2] The President says this in order to blame his own 1970-72 recession on the peace he claims he is bringing to Vietnam and to justify his New Economic Policy as paving the way for an unprecedented era of combined peace and prosperity.

Proponents of the Marxist-Nixon position can point to the political barriers to expansion of civilian spending in the first Kennedy–Johnson Administration, and note that otherwise firm taboos on deficit spending could be broken for the Berlin build-up in 1961 and the Vietnam escalation later.

On the other hand, recovery to full employment was virtually complete in 1965 prior to the escalation of war spending. The unemployment rate was 4.5% and declining in July 1965 before President Johnson announced

---

[2] On the most recent occasion, one of his advisers apparently told him to except the Eisenhower boom of 1955-57.

the Vietnam build-up. By year's end it was down to 4.1%. In the last half of 1965 defense purchases rose at an annual rate of $2 billion per quarter. These outlays cannot account for the increases in employment, but it could be argued that business investment in response to actual and prospective defense orders made up the difference. Through July 1965, perhaps longer, defense was not supporting the recovery. After the 1961 Berlin bulge, defense spending actually declined in the years 1962-65 and reached the lowest fraction of potential GNP since before Korea. Even at its recent peak in 1968, the defense share of capacity output was smaller than in the "peacetime" years of 1953-58.

Federal nondefense purchases, in contrast, rose by $7.2 billion (75%) from 1961 to 1965, and transfers to persons and state and local governments by $9.3 billion (29%). Subsequent increases, from 1965 to 1971, in federal civilian outlays were even more substantial: $9.4 billion (56%) in purchases and $61.7 (149%) in transfers. Evidently the neo-Marxist analysis underrates the political acceptability of civilian spending. A more amazing oversight is the possibility of tax cuts, a means of getting money spent without competing with private enterprise or raising the supply price of unskilled labor.

This omission is related to a similar error in the standard Marxist explanation of the superior performance of the American economy after the Second World War as compared to the Great Depression. The explanation is the immensely higher defense budget, which the Marxists and New Leftists interpret not as a response to the Cold War but as its economically caused source. They overlook the fact that federal tax revenues also had to be vastly increased to neutralize the demand stimulus of the defense budgets. Otherwise aggregate demand would have been hopelessly and chronically excessive.

Postwar prosperity obviously did not require defense spending on anything like the scale observed. That fact leaves postwar defense spending, both its general level and its fluctuations, to be explained on other than Marxist-Keynesian grounds. One alternative is the self-interest and political clout of defense contractors, subcontractors, and workers and the cozy relationships they built up with the Pentagon. Eisenhower's "military-industrial complex" labels the phenomenon, and Galbraith has elaborated its description. I do not doubt that this phenomenon explains some billions of dollars. Nevertheless we do observe cutbacks in defense spending, overall and in particular lines, bringing distress to the stockholders and employees of defense businesses.

As for the general ups and downs of the defense budget, a naive explanation in terms of responses to world events fits the facts very well. Figure 1 shows defense spending in percent of potential GNP in relation to major crises in international relations since 1945.

It is true that the postwar size of the federal budget has made economic stabilization an easier task than it was before 1940. A large budget contributes to built-in stability because it entails higher tax rates, and higher tax rates mean a lower Keynesian multiplier. Consequently exogenous shocks to aggregate demand have less effect. The other side of this coin is the heavy drag that high tax rates exert on expansion of demand.

44

A large budget also facilitates discretionary fiscal policy. It is clearly easier to make budgetary changes equivalent to 1% of GNP now, when the budget is 20% of GNP, than in 1929, when it was only 3½% of GNP. Since the multiplier was higher in 1929, it was not necessary to make as large budget changes relative to GNP to achieve the same total GNP effect. But this offset would be complete only if the economy's marginal propensity to spend from income after taxes were as high as unity. If that marginal propensity were .8 and marginal tax shares were equal to average, the 1972 multiplier would be 63% as large as the 1929 multiplier, whereas the 1972 budget is 5.7 times as big in relation to GNP. In relation to the size of the budget, the change needed for given GNP impact would have been 3.6 times as big in 1929.

These stabilization dividends of large defense spending were certainly unintended. And now, without defense, federal outlays are 13% of GNP, plenty big enough for stabilization, built-in and discretionary. In addition, there is always monetary policy, and no one contends that a large defense budget is essential to the Federal Reserve.

A second set of charges also relates to the intersection of economics and war, but with a different twist. Did the New Economics abet the war? In her Ely Lecture at the convention of the American Economic Association in December 1971, entitled "The Second Crisis of Economic Theory," Joan Robinson accused American Keynesians of learning too well that government spending could sustain full employment.[3] They learned the lesson

[3] *American Economic Review*, LXII. May 1972 Proceedings. 1-18.

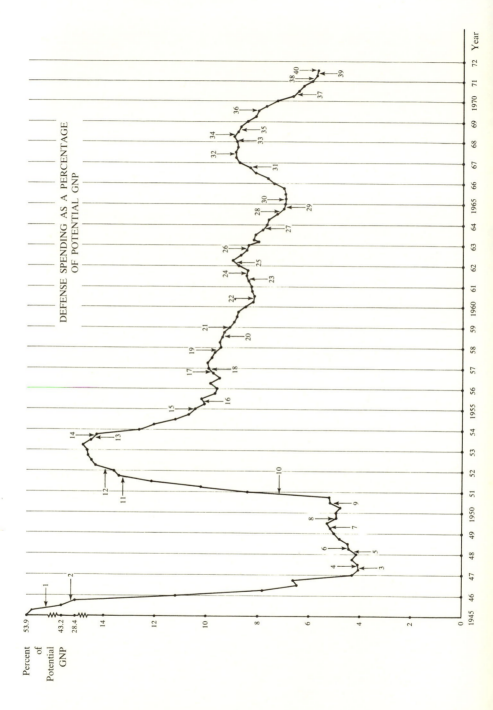

DEFENSE SPENDING AS A PERCENTAGE
OF POTENTIAL GNP

Key to Figure

1945		
1.	May 7	Germany surrenders
2.	September 2	Japan surrenders
1947		
3.	May 22	Aid to Greece and Turkey under the Truman Doctrine
4.	June 5	Marshall proposes the Marshall Plan at Harvard
1948		
5.	February 25	Czechoslovakia joins the Communist Bloc
6.	April 1	Land blockade of Berlin by the Soviets
	" 3	Foreign Assistance Act of 1948 enacted (Marshall Plan)
1949		
7.	April 4	NATO Treaty signed
8.	September 23	Truman announces that USSR possesses the atomic bomb
	October 1	Communist China is proclaimed
1950		
9.	June 25	North Korean troops invade South Korea
	" 30	Truman authorizes ground troops in Korea
10.	November 20	US troops at the Manchurian border
	" 29	Retreat of US troops
1951		
11.	July 10	First Korean peace talks

so well, she said, that they welcomed indiscriminately any kind of spending, with no thought of allocational priorities. In particular they welcomed defense and war spending.

Other critics have pointed out that liberation from the balanced budget fetish frees political leaders to spend for Vietnam wars, as well as for Great Societies, without the test of taxpayer approval. Robert Eisner thought that the Johnson Administration should be denied the techniques and expertise of the New Economics; he called on the Council to resign. On the other hand, a number of economists opposed President Johnson's belated tax surcharge proposal, on the ground that his marginal propensity to spend tax receipts for war was significantly positive. Presumably they believed that deficit spending for the war would be limited by the Administration's fear of inflationary consequences.

Mrs. Robinson's charge against American economic thought is ridiculous. That very American neo-classical synthesis which she criticizes on other occasions stresses that there are many routes to full employment and that no one use of idle resources can be justified simply because it uses idle resources. As I have argued above, neither the economy nor the New Economists needed the Vietnam War for full employment. As for the complaint that Keynesians taught governments how to spend for war without taxing, it is comparable to the view that sex education is to be blamed for the fact that teenagers learn about sex. Government bonds and printing presses were invented before the New Economics, and budget orthodoxy never prevented their use in wartime.

1952	12.	January 24	Deadlock at Korean peace talks
1953	13.	July 27	Korean armistice
	14.	August 20	USSR explodes its own H Bomb
1955	15.	January 1	US begins financial aid to S.E. Asia
		" 1	Eisenhower pledges US to defense of Formosa and the Pescadores
1956	16.	May 14	Warsaw Pact formed
	17.	October 29	Israel invades Sinai Peninsula
	18.	November 4	Hungarian revolt crushed by Soviets
1957	19.	October 4	Soviets launch Sputnik I
1958	20.	July 15	US sends troops to Lebanon
1959	21.	January 1	Castro comes to power in Cuba
1960	22.	May 5	U-2 shot down over USSR, pilot Gary Powers
		" 10	Khrushchev uses U-2 incident to kill Paris Summit Conference
1961	23.	April 17	Bay of Pigs invasion
	24.	August 12	East Germany raises the Berlin Wall
1962	25.	February 14	President authorizes US troops in Vietnam to fire at enemy only for self-protection
	26.	October 22	Cuban missile quarantine
1963	27.	October 11	USSR blocks American military convoy going to West Berlin
		November 7	Overthrow of Diem, US supports provisional government in South Vietnam
1964	28.	August 2	Gulf of Tonkin incident
	29.	October 16	Communist China explodes its first atomic bomb
1965	30.	March 8	US marines land in South Vietnam
1966	31.	July 1	France withdraws all forces from NATO
1967	32.	June 5-10	Arab-Israeli War
1968	33.	January 23	North Korea seizes the *Pueblo*
		" 30	Tet offensive
	34.	May 10	Preliminary peace talks on Vietnam
	35.	August 20	Soviets invade Czechoslovakia
1969	36.	July 8	First troop withdrawal from Vietnam
1970	37.	April 30	US incursion into Cambodia
1971	38.	February 8	South Vietnamese enter Laos
	39.	May 3	Senate bars reduction in NATO forces proposed by Senator Mansfield
	40.	July 15	Nixon announces China visit

Should economists leave a government in protest of noneconomic policies which they play no part in determining, administering, or defending? This is quite a different issue, one of personal commitments and beliefs. Surely the economists had no professional obligation to quit, and no special obligation greater than that of any other public servants. Even if they privately opposed the war, they could ask themselves whether any national interest, including the end of the war, would be furthered by failing to manage as well as possible its impact on the economy. It is a different issue whether they should have resigned when their professional advice was rejected, comparable to the issue facing George Ball, a dissenter on Vietnam, whether he should resign from the State Department. Every adviser knows that his advice is not always taken and faces a difficult calculation whether he does more good inside or outside government.

The New Economics and National Priorities

A third charge brought against the New Economics is neglect of the civilian public sector in favor of tax reductions to stimulate private spending. I discussed this criticism in the first chapter, and earlier in this one I cited the record of substantial increase in federal civilian spending. Actually the criticism, justified or not, is more a rebuke to the New Economists of the Kennedy–Johnson Administrations than to New Economics as a body of macro-economic doctrine. The doctrine itself is neutral as to size of the public sector and as to the choice between taxes and expenditures as vehicles of fiscal policy.

51

The New Economics is also accused of indifference to the inequality of income and wealth. Again this is more a rebuke to individual advisers than to doctrine per se. In response they could point to a number of proposals, some adopted, many not. The war on poverty, after all, was an initiative of Walter Heller and his Council. Tax reforms proposed to Congress in 1961-62 included withholding of tax on interest and dividends, limits on deductible expense accounts, and stiffer taxation of foreign earnings of U.S. corporations. Unfortunately, the only major result was to require information reports by payers of interest and dividends. Further reforms were proposed in 1963-64, but only two important ones survived—the minimum standard deduction and the repeal of the dividend credit. Medicare and Medicaid, let us not forget, were enacted under President Johnson.

The enumeration could continue, but it would not gainsay the essential validity of the complaint. To state it another way, liberal Democratic administrations in the 1960s did not undertake major redistributive crusades in the traditions of Bryan, Wilson, and the two Roosevelts. The approach of the sixties was rather consensus politics, emphasizing programs that could draw support or at least acquiescence from most major economic interests. This was partly a reflection of the political balance of the nation; I have already noted how vulnerable President Kennedy and his Administration felt on inauguration day. It was partly an outgrowth of President Kennedy's feeling, expressed in his 1962 Yale Commencement address, that the solutions of many national problems were blocked more by irrational ideology than by real conflict of interest and could be found by removing ideological blinders to dispassionate pragmatic analysis. He was right, but he exaggerated. No one can know, but I believe that, buttressed by the popularity he had earned before his death and by the decisive victory he would have won in 1964, he would have been ready to lead a crusade for social justice. His successor, we know, was addicted to consensus politics, and the promise of Johnson's Great Society was aborted by the tragedy of Vietnam.

The practitioners of the New Economics did not have to confront distributive issues squarely. It was apparent in advance that if their macro-economic policies took effect and succeeded, recovery and growth during the 1960s would do much more to lift the incomes of the poor and disadvantaged than any conceivable redistribution and would be much less politically and socially divisive. This was not only apparent in advance; it is true in retrospect. Our acquiescence to liberalized depreciation and sponsorship of the investment tax credit, in the interests of investment and growth, can be faulted on distributional grounds, especially as compensating tax reforms like limiting deductible personal and entertainment expenses vanished in the legislative process. The original form of the investment tax credit as proposed by Council and Treasury economists confined the credit to investment *net* of depreciation. This would have been much less a giveaway, more desirable on grounds of efficiency (the credit on gross investment encouraged

53

less durable investments), and at least as great an incentive. But this feature, as probably should have been expected, slipped away in Congressional committee.

Although some New Economists in and out of government have actively promoted the negative income tax, I was disappointed that the Johnson Administration, largely because of opposition in the Department of Health, Education, and Welfare, never officially endorsed it. Joseph Pechman's American Finance Association Presidential Address in December 1971 demonstrates dramatically the horizontal inequity and the lack of effective progressivity in current personal income taxation. Likewise, estate taxation in this country permits altogether too much inequality to be perpetuated by inheritance. I should like to see the egalitarian values of many of today's young people translated into a militant crusade for a decent income guarantee financed by progressive reform of income and estate taxation.

Another criticism of the New Economics is that it emphasized economic growth, which more and more people now regard as curse rather than blessing. It is hard for me to understand how any of America's current social and ecological problems would have been avoided or ameliorated by halting growth in 1961. Advocates of Zero Economic Growth should specify just how their proposal would be implemented. To produce 1960 output in 1969 would have required roughly a third fewer manhours than were actually employed in 1969. To produce 1960 per capita output in 1969 would have taken a fifth fewer manhours. Unless there were compulsory reductions of hours of work, ZEG beginning in 1960 would have meant unemployment on the order of 25-30% of the labor force by 1969, 15-20% if per capita output had been maintained. The unemployment might be disguised and spread by reducing hours of work to about 24 per week, or 30 by the per capita standard. But the population does not want all that leisure, so the ZEG statute would have to forbid moonlighting. Moreover, the uses of compulsory leisure might well turn out to be as damaging to the environment as the production and consumption foregone.

Of course the embarrassing increase in the economy's productivity could be prevented by suppressing technological progress and capital investment. How does a society go about prohibiting technological progress? Is all technological progress ecologically harmful? Would the environment be saved by consuming 100% of whatever output is produced? To ask such questions is to demonstrate the absurdity of the whole aggregative anti-growth movement. Contrary to its expressed premises, economic growth does not occur because economists worship GNP. In all humility we economists must confess that the contribution of economic policy to growth rates is quite small. Nor does economic growth occur simply or even principally because greedy manufacturers brainwash consumers to buy more and more things they do not really want. At best or worst their efforts alter patterns of consumption and marginally retard the trend toward shorter hours of work. The main culprit is technological progress.

The answer to environmental problems is not a sledge-hammer suppression of overall GNP but a series of

55

attacks specifically targeted on the particular technologies and activities that damage the environment. A halt to growth would not eliminate urban congestion, automobile emissions, burning of sulphur-bearing oil to generate power, runoff of detergents and fertilizers into lakes, tanker oil spills, or pollution of rivers by industrial and human waste. The growth rate of these evils since the war has been orders of magnitude greater than that of GNP. The remedy is in principle well known to economists: namely, to charge specific production and consumption activities for the social damage they do. A proper costing system will change the directions of economic growth. It may as by-product diminish our customary measures of overall growth, but that is not the purpose.[4]

The Kennedy–Johnson Administrations and their economic advisers can be chided for a late start in this area, but they need not apologize for the economy's overall growth. It would be silly to deprive ourselves of growth in the directions of health care and education and housing because automobiles pollute the air and congest the streets. It is not likely that a technologically and economically stagnant society is going to generate either the techniques or the resources to solve its ecological problems.

Everyone agrees that population, even in North America, must some day be stabilized. I suppose no one is

[4] For a discussion of the relation between economic growth and welfare and an attempt to develop a welfare-oriented measure of economic activity, see William Nordhaus and James Tobin, *Is Growth Obsolete?*, National Bureau of Economic Research, Fiftieth Anniversary, Colloquium, V, 1972.

blaming the New Economics for population growth over the last decade—so far as I know, no economists have wanted to maximize GNP growth by maximizing birth rates. Likewise, I suppose no one is crediting the New Economics for the dramatic decline in age-standardized birth rates over the last decade. Fortunately, it seems that present trends will bring Zero Population Growth to this country without any policy more drastic than facilitating the avoidance of undesired births. Demographic forecasts are as faulty as economic projections, and the demand for children may turn up again. Meanwhile we seem to be in the happy position that we need neither to restrict free choice nor to penalize children once born in order to induce mothers to bear fewer.

Economists of my generation grew up in the Depression and learned economics at the birth of the Keynesian Revolution. We were attracted to the subject by the happy combination of intellectual excitement and promise of dramatic social improvement. Massive unemployment, economic stagnation, instability and insecurity were far-reaching evils, but ones that human intelligence could overcome. Sometimes, no doubt, we romantically exaggerated the contributions of full employment and economic progress to economic welfare and social harmony. Anyway, we know now that prosperity does not eliminate waste, injustice, poverty, conflict, crime, and war. It is natural for younger economists to underrate problems already more or less solved and to emphasize those that remain. But it is an overreaction to conclude that past focus on growth and full employment actually created the remaining problems or made them worse.

The Monetarist Challenge

I turn now to an attack from a different direction, monetarism, which challenged not the values and priorities of the New Economics but its understanding of economic mechanism. The New Economics, in its view, was not so much evil and blind as stupid and wrong. When the New Economics stumbled over Vietnam and fell from public favor, monetarism was waiting in the wings and burst upon the scene. The press thrives upon drama, conflict, and novelty. These were the same attributes that made the New Economics newsworthy in the earlier sixties, and now they favored the propagation of monetarism. Here was a doctrine that had formidable but heterodox academic credentials, claimed to forecast GNP accurately and simply, fixed blame for the unpleasant oscillations in the economy after 1965, alleged that both monetary and fiscal policy had been based on false economics, and asserted that fine-tuning caused or accentuated the instability it was designed to correct.

Monetarism, in my understanding of it, encompasses the following propositions: (a) Past rates of growth in the stock of money are the major determinants—indeed, virtually the only systematic, nonrandom determinants—of the growth of nominal (current-dollar) GNP. (b) A corollary: Fiscal policies do not significantly affect nominal GNP, though they may alter its composition and also affect interest rates. (c) Another corollary: The overall impact on nominal GNP of monetary and financial policies and events is for practical purposes summed up in the movements of a single variable, the stock of money.

58

Consequently monetary policy should be exclusively guided by this variable, to the exclusion of interest rates, credit flows, free reserves, and other indicators. (d) Nominal interest rates are geared to inflation expectations and thus, with a lag, to actual inflation. Although the immediate market impact of expansionary monetary policy may be to lower interest rates, this is fairly soon reversed when premiums for the resulting inflation are added to interest rates. (e) The central bank can and should make the money stock grow at a steady rate equal to the rate of growth of potential GNP plus a target rate of inflation. (f) There is no enduring trade-off between unemployment and inflation but rather a unique natural rate of unemployment that allows for structural change and job search. Government policy will produce ever-accelerating inflation if it persistently seeks a lower than natural rate of unemployment and an ever-accelerating deflation if it seeks a higher rate. If the proper steady-growth monetary policy is followed, the economy will settle into its natural unemployment rate. Since this equilibrium can be achieved with any rate of inflation, the inflation target might as well be zero.

In their more defensive moments monetarists seek to disarm their critics by reducing their message to "money matters" or "monetary policy is important." Such simple, vague, and uncontroversial propositions do not begin to do their doctrines justice and cannot support their policy prescriptions. Almost no one nowadays—certainly none of the practitioners or exponents of the New Economics—contends that money does not matter and that monetary policy is irrelevant to the course of nominal GNP.

Keynes himself did not believe that—quite the contrary. He did point out the theoretical possibility of a liquidity trap, where aggregate demand would be unresponsive to monetary policies. Relevant interest rates would already be so low that the banks and public, with no incentive to economize money holdings, would simply hold idle any additional money provided by the central bank. He regarded the trap as a practical possibility in the depths of the Great Depression but certainly not a normal condition. Some empirical studies at the time cast doubt on the responsiveness of business spending to interest rate movements within the narrow ranges of Depression experience. In their *Monetary History of the United States, 1867-1960*,[5] Friedman and Schwartz challenge Keynesian interpretations of the Depression and argue that monetary policy was effective for good or ill even then. Whatever the merits of that challenge, they have nothing to do with postwar economics.

Some Keynesians, it is true, carried their Depression skepticism of monetary policy into the postwar years. This mistake was more common in the United Kingdom than in this country. The Radcliffe Report of 1959[6] and the writings of Nicholas Kaldor until this very day provide monetarists with British targets that are neither ancient nor wholly straw. In the United States standard neo-Keynesian doctrine, that neo-classical synthesis I

[5] National Bureau of Economic Research, *Studies in Business Cycles* No. 12 (Princeton: Princeton University Press, 1963).
[6] *Op. cit.*

have previously cited, has allowed money an important role at least since 1950, long before the rise of monetarism. Government policy has proceeded on the same view at least since the Treasury–Federal Reserve Accord of 1951.

Nothing could be more misleading, therefore, than to characterize the contemporary debate in the United States as one between "monetarists" and "fiscalists." The debate is not symmetrical. By symmetry to the monetarist propositions I listed above, a fiscalist would claim that only fiscal policy matters, money is irrelevant, and so forth. There are no such fiscalists. The only extremists are monetarists. The press has done great disservice to its interested readers by uncritically retailing to them a biased and inaccurate description of the controversy.

There cannot even be a meaningful debate over which is more effective or important, fiscal or monetary policy. Any comparison of the effectiveness of two medicines requires a common metric for the dosages. There can be no meaningful common measures except in terms of costs and side effects. Comparing the GNP effects of a billion dollars of open market purchases with those of a billion dollars of full employment deficit is about as useful as comparing competing drugs on the basis of pain relief per pill.

As for importance, there can be meaningful empirical investigation of how much of the actual variation of nominal GNP over a historical period is statistically explained by monetary variables, and how much by fiscal variables. The results will be ambiguous unless the two

61

kinds of variables happened to vary independently over the sample period. Otherwise they depend on which variables are treated as marginal; if they always move together, either one can be credited with the full explanation and the other with nothing. Anyway, the failure of a policy variable to contribute a great deal to historical explanation does not necessarily signify ineffectiveness. It may mean simply that the variable changed very little during the period of observation.

Returning to the list of monetarist propositions, observe that they are not all logically linked. One may accept some and reject others. For example, a believer in the potency of monetary policy to the exclusion of fiscal policy need not buy the stock of money as a sufficient indicator. Many nonmonetarists are adherents of the "natural rate" alternative to the Phillips trade-off. A subscriber to the monetarist model of economic mechanism is not compelled to conclude that no policymaking procedure utilizing information fed back from the economy can do better than a fixed rate of growth of the money stock. And so on.

Why, then, are these propositions considered a package? The only answer is that they all happen to be propounded by the redoubtable monetarist leader, Milton Friedman. His personality, combined with the historical accident that the ancient quantity theory was kept alive through dark decades at the University of Chicago, is also the only available explanation of why monetarism is predominantly a right-wing phenomenon.

There is no inherent logic that places monetarists to the right of New Economists. They have different models of economic mechanism, but they need not have different political values. A conservative can be a Keynesian and a liberal a monetarist. These combinations are in fact surprisingly rare. Is it that people who favor a large public sector are naturally disposed to believe in the efficacy of fiscal policy for economic stabilization, whereas advocates of small government are disposed to downgrade it? This may make sense if one believes that the public sector will expand as increases in public spending are regularly used to promote cyclical recoveries while tax increases or high interest rates are used to check booms. But it is no less plausible that the threat of inflation is a publicly persuasive argument against bigger budgets, one that is lost if the monetarists are right that the budget doesn't matter. Is there any particular reason why monetarism has special appeal to enthusiasts for free markets or to those whose political philosophy leads them to advocate rules in place of discretionary authority? Given that the government budget and taxes are there anyway, fiscal policy involves no more market intervention than monetary policy, probably less. And it is at least equally susceptible of being subject to a fixed rule, such as a constant full employment budget surplus.

This is not the occasion for a theoretical and empirical critique of the monetarist propositions, a topic on which I have not been silent in the past.[7] Most of the main points come up in the historical context of this book—

[7] See my *Essays in Economics, Volume I: Macroeconomics* (Chicago: Markham, 1972), Chaps. 23 and 24, and "Friedman's Theoretical Framework," *Journal of Political Economy*, LXXX, No. 5 (Sept./Oct. 1972), 852-63.

namely, in the controversy over the sources of the expansion of the 1960s, in particular after the 1964 tax cut.

The New Economics interpretation is the following: The tax cut, as well as the lesser fiscal stimuli that preceded it, worked pretty much as multiplier theory predicts, even better because the expansion of GNP induced investment as well as consumption. The Federal Reserve at the time was following a policy best described as "bill rate only." That is, there was a bill rate floor related to foreign interest rates; any lower rate, it was feared, would drive funds abroad. In somewhat lesser degree the floor was also a ceiling. In a slack noninflationary economy the Fed was willing to meet expanding demands for bank reserves at the target rate rather than let interest rates rise. As the recovery, fueled by fiscal policy and other nonmonetary stimuli, increased demands for money and bank reserves, the Fed provided the supplies. Every so often the target bill rate was raised a quarter or half point, but the Fed was not leaning against the wind with the weight customary in the fifties. A less accommodating monetary policy would have slowed down the expansion, but even constancy in money stock or unborrowed reserves relative to potential GNP would not have cut it off altogether. So goes the New Economics interpretation.

The monetarist interpretation is quite different: The GNP expansion did not cause, but was caused by, the growth of money supply and bank reserves. The tax cut was irrelevant. Maybe the financing of federal deficits provided occasions for monetary injections, motivated by the cosmetics of debt management. The same injections could have occurred, with the same effects, without the deficits. The modest rise in interest rates was due to federal financing, induced investment, and heightened expectations of inflation.

The conflicting interpretations exemplify the problem of identification that plagues econometrics. But there are some clues that favor the New Economics version. First and most important, both direct observation and Federal Open Market Committee minutes support the view that the Fed was supplying an indeterminate quantity of reserves at periodically fixed interest rates rather than making autonomously determined increments in monetary aggregates. Indeed, Friedman and other monetarists bitterly criticized the Fed precisely for its wrongheaded pursuit of interest-rate rather than quantitative targets. This monetarist criticism is inconsistent with monetarist econometrics, here and in other applications. If the Fed has misbehaved as charged, monetarist statisticians have no right to treat the money stock as exogenous in their regressions.

The second point concerns the definition of the money stock. Monetarists are fuzzy and fickle in identifying the monetary aggregate that possesses the magical properties their strong propositions attribute to the stock of "money." One might expect the concept to follow from a theory specifying the unique and distinctive properties of money. Instead we are told that choice among various monetary aggregates is seldom a practical issue because they generally move together. Anyway, it is a question for empirical inquiry rather than prior analysis. In the period under review they did not move together. Table 1 gives percentage increases for various candidates over the whole pre-Vietnam recovery period and over the two years of it affected by the tax cut. For reference it also gives the percentage increase of nominal GNP in the first six months of the subsequent years.

TABLE 1

Percentage Increases in Monetary Aggregates (end of year) and Nominal GNP (first half of succeeding year)

	1960-65	*1963-65*
M_1: conventional money supply, i.e., currency plus demand deposits	19	9
M_1 augmented by time and savings deposits in commercial banks	47	18
M_1 augmented by all time and savings deposits and shares	53	19
Unborrowed bank reserves	16	9
Nominal GNP	44	19

The third point is the behavior of velocity. As Table 1 indicates, the GNP velocity of the conventional money supply, M_1, shot up in the sixties. This was not the continuation of a trend. Between 1951 and 1959 velocity rose from 2.75 to 3.16; by 1965 it was 4.17, and 4.41 in the next year. The New Economics explanation runs in terms of the incentive that interest rates on other available liquid assets give for economizing money balances. Logically the strong monetarist propositions cannot stand up if velocity is sensitive to interest rates, for if fiscal policy and other nonmonetary stimuli can raise interest rates and velocity, they can raise nominal GNP without any monetary expansion. Friedman has resisted this logic

66

and claimed that the whole issue is irrelevant, but he has hedged his bets by empirical findings that the interest-sensitivity of velocity is negligible. He is alone among empirical investigators of the demand for money in reaching this conclusion; observed pro-cyclical movements of velocity are hard to explain without interest rates.[8]

The usual monetarist scenario for a cyclical recovery driven by monetary expansion implies that velocity will not rise but fall. Suppose that growth rates of money are increased and nominal GNP follows with a distributed lag. During the monetary expansion velocity will be declining. In the period under review, as previously noted, velocity increased. Interest rates gradually rose, as the Fed successively tightened the screw to keep mobile dollars at home. The rise in rates on liquid substitutes for demand deposits explains the large increases in time and savings deposits in commercial banks and thrift institutions, exhibited in Table 1.

On these grounds I must, not surprisingly, move for a verdict in favor of the New Economics interpretation as against the monetarist interpretation.

The tax surcharge of 1968 provides a stronger case against the effectiveness of fiscal policy. The surcharge was oversold during the long delay preceding its enactment. Both the Administration and the Fed overestimated its potency and underrated the momentum of the economy following the "growth recession" of 1967. Their very success in limiting the duration and extent of that

---

[8] As pointed out by Arthur M. Okun, *The Political Economy of Prosperity* (Washington, D.C.: Brookings Institution, 1970), pp. 58-59 and 146-47, where a catalog of these investigations is given.

slowdown convinced business investors that the economy could and would be held close to the full employment growth track. Given that conviction, inflation considerably diluted the deterrent effects of historically high nominal interest rates. In what we can now see was unjustified fear that the surcharge would be too deflationary, the Fed eased up on the monetary brakes in mid-1968.

On the same superficial test by which the 1964 tax cut was generally perceived to be a success—conformity of subsequent events to advance claims—the 1968 surcharge was a failure. It is also true that monetarists would not have made this mistake, since they would not have expected anything from the surcharge in the first place.

I think the exaggerated hope for the surcharge had quite different roots. The division of disposable income between consumption and saving is very volatile from quarter to quarter and year to year. Our capacity to predict the personal saving ratio is very limited, but differences of one half or one percentage point (3½ or 7 billion dollars in today's economy) are the equivalent of substantial changes in government spending or private investment. Thanks to affluence and modern consumer credit arrangements, fewer and fewer households are forced by sheer liquidity constraints to gear their spending to their cash receipts. They have wide scope for rearranging the timing of their purchases, and how they do so depends on their moods and expectations. Unlike the 1964 tax cut, the surcharge was specified to be temporary, to expire in twelve months. Households free of liquidity constraints had plenty of room to adjust their consumption to long-range estimates of their consumable resources. The apparent failure of consumption to re-spond—the dramatic fall in the ratio of personal saving to disposable income—could be explained in those terms.

But I am not arguing so much for a mechanical application of permanent income or life cycle calculation as for humility in short-run consumption forecasting and caution in predicting tax effects from conventional liquidity-oriented consumption functions. I am aware of Arthur Okun's simulation study showing that the surcharge did about what the consumption functions of econometric models would predict.[9] Those equations, then, could not justify the advance claims for the surcharge. Moreover, insofar as they show the fall in the saving ratio following the surcharge as a return to normality rather than an effect of the surcharge itself, they were evidently under-estimating the saving ratio and overestimating consumption in the preceding quarters. I shall say something about the policy implications of this episode in the final chapter.

Neither theory nor fact prevented the monetarist tide from eroding the intellectual support of the New Economics in the economics profession itself and in Congress, the Federal Reserve, the banking and financial community, and the press. Nevertheless, now that the monetarist tide is waning, I must conclude that little lasting harm has been done, unless the time of economists on both sides is heavily valued.

With prodding from the Joint Economic Committee, the Federal Open Market Committee began to include

[9] Arthur Okun, "The Personal Tax Surcharge and Consumer Demand," *Brookings Papers on Economic Activity*, 1971, No. 1, pp. 167-211.

a money stock target in its monthly directive, at least as a contingent limit on the operations of the "desk." Certainly the rate of growth of the money stock has become the customary capsule form for describing monetary policy and gauging how easy or tight it is. For a time it seemed that public preoccupation with this number might by itself be a market constraint on the Federal Reserve. Believers in monetarism would regard accelerated growth of M_1 as the harbinger of more inflation and higher interest rates. If such people were to dominate financial markets, they would make it difficult for the Fed to carry out a rate-reducing expansionary policy. Fortunately, the Fed has not taken too seriously the fears that monetarism might be a self-fulfilling prophecy. The Fed has rightly paid attention to fluctuations in the demand for money. It has understood that accommodating greater liquidity preference was not inflationary in early 1971 even though money stock growth rates were large, and that low money stock growth rates were not per se deflationary in late 1971 when asset preferences shifted the other way.

At the beginning of the Nixon Administration there were indications that the new Council and other top economists were taking a monetarist line. The adoption of balance in the full employment budget as a fixed rule seemed almost to abandon discretionary fiscal policy. But events, common sense, and politics have prevailed. In 1972 the Administration proudly pointed to a fiscal deficit, even in the full employment budget, as its principal weapon to promote recovery and reduce unemployment. The New Economics lives after all.

70

3

Prospects for Macro-Economic Policy

IN this country, as in others, the central government has gradually assumed political responsibility for the overall performance of the economy. Today the electorate does not fatalistically accept business cycles, unemployment, and inflation as acts of nature. Incumbent administrations and opposition candidates are expected to have programs to do something about them. Presidents are judged by their economic statistics.

Before the Great Depression, certainly before the First World War, macro-economic issues were much less central. There were plenty of economic issues in political campaigns, but they were sectional and distributional, like the complaints of Western farmers against Eastern financiers, or of workers and consumers against big business. These issues still exist, but in addition federal governments are accountable for their stewardship as managers of a vast enterprise, the U.S. economy.

This accountability was formalized in the Employment Act of 1946, and during the last decade public policy and debate have fixed it still more firmly. The New Economics contributed to this trend, as I argued in the preceding chapters, by raising the sights of stabilization policy, by setting more precise and definite targets, and

71

by clearing away some ancient ideological obstacles to the full dedication of monetary and fiscal policy to economic ends. The New Economics advocated and, in a large degree, carried out an activist policy for stabilization; if it wasn't fine-tuning, the dials weren't locked either.

Have the public's standards of performance outrun the capabilities of policymakers? Is the government now responsible for more than it can reasonably be expected to deliver? Does it have enough, and good enough, tools? What lessons can we learn from the last decade? In this final chapter I propose to offer some reflections on these questions, although I could not begin to answer them fully even if I had much more time.

Policy with and without Feedback

First, let us consider the recommendation that the government eschew active stabilization policy in favor of an automatic fixed rule. This recommendation, as I observed in the second chapter, is generally associated with monetarism; and the rule recommended is a steady rate of growth, perhaps month to month, certainly quarter to quarter, in the stock of money. (I should say "*a* stock of money," given the abundance of candidates for the honor.) But there is no logical necessity to link the recommendation of a fixed rule to monetarism, or to confine it to monetary policy. There are other possible fixed rules for monetary policy: for example, a pegged interest rate, a constant rate of growth of bank reserves, a certain percentage of net free to required reserves. A fixed rule for fiscal policy might be a full employment budget surplus growing at a steady rate, or constant as a percentage of potential GNP.

The distinctive characteristic of a fixed rule is that policy is independent of feedback. Observations of the current or past state of the economy, guesses and forecasts of the future, are conscientiously ignored. Policymakers do not pay any attention to how far and in what direction they are missing their targets.

Information from feedback is the essence of successful control mechanisms, driving a car, heating a house, guiding a space craft, and the like. Why should makers of economic policy ignore it? The presumption, after all, is that information can do no harm; at the worst it simply doesn't help. In economic systems the evidence is that deviations of variables from relationships estimated from past experience have high positive serial correlation. Consequently these errors are useful information for the policymaker. He will not be wrong to take them into account in adjusting his aim. Simulation experiments with macro-econometric models, including the monetarist model of the St. Louis Federal Reserve Bank, show that policies based on feedback perform better than fixed rules.[1]

But what if the policymakers do not know the structure of the system they are trying to control? We all know examples of incompetent controllers who destabilize the

[1] J. Phillip Cooper and Stanley Fischer, "Stochastic Simulation of Monetary Rules in Two Macroeconometric Models," *Journal of the American Statistical Association*, LXVII, No. 340 (Dec. 1972), 750-60.

systems they are trying to stabilize—the impatient knob-turner in the shower who alternately scalds and freezes, the foolish housewife who can't leave the thermostat alone, and so on. The same thing might happen to the economy if policymakers responded to every observed discrepancy from target by taking action theoretically strong enough to eliminate it, ignoring the lags before their current and past actions have full effect. This is conceivable, but so serious a recommendation should be based on more than a possibility.

Advocates of a fixed rule allege that government itself has been the main source of destabilizing shocks to the economy. If wars are counted, this is surely true; consider Vietnam and Korea, to say nothing of the world wars. Both Korea and Vietnam had their initial impact through the expectations and spending propensities of private citizens. Rules relating to government monetary and fiscal policy would not have prevented the fall-winter booms of 1950-51 and 1965-66. A fiscal rule would have required and possibly made more likely tax increases in 1966.

Anyway, the destabilizing effects of war are far from showing that government actions for purposes of stabilization have been destabilizing. Are there examples in recent history of government behaving like an idiot shower-taker or foolish furnace-tender? There are long decision lags in fiscal policy, as the 1964 tax cut and the 1968 surcharge remind us. In spite of the delays, both measures were still appropriate at the time they were passed. Possibly the belated suspension of the investment tax credit in October 1966 is an example of a badly timed

fiscal decision. As for monetary policy, the major error in retrospect was excessive ease in 1967 and 1968, contributing to the renewal of inflationary boom in 1968 and 1969. But this was not a naive error of timing, a failure to understand lags in response. Instead it was an attempt to anticipate fiscal restraints that were delayed much longer and were weaker in effect than expected. I do not blame monetary expansion in 1965 and early 1966 for the overheating of 1966, because I am confident that following a monetarist rule would not have prevented Vietnam from bringing about a big rise in monetary velocity.

The Nixon game plan before August 1971 can be criticized for slowness in shifting gears to expansionary policy. But the long recession was not the unintended carryover of disinflationary measures taken too late in the preceding boom. Rather it was deliberate policy to wait for clear signs that the stubborn inflation was abating.

The monetarist rule itself involves some policy response to feedback information, but the information relates to an intermediate variable rather than to the variables the Fed is trying to control. The rule does not prescribe fixed settings of the instruments the Federal Reserve directly controls, like the unborrowed reserve base of the banking system. Rather the Fed is asked to offset changes in bank and public behavior that alter the relation of the chosen monetary aggregate to the reserve base, while ignoring information fed back—in interest rates, credit flows, velocity statistics—about changes in behavior that alter the relation of the money stock to the

ultimate target variables. It takes a strange and special model of the economy to justify complete response to the one type of feedback and zero response to the other.

Making Fiscal Policy More Flexible

I turn now to the adequacy of the tools of stabilization policy. Experience over the last decade and ongoing developments in the U.S. and world economy provide good reasons for concern on this score. We must try to sharpen our fiscal and monetary tools.

In fiscal policy in the United States the main problems arise from the separation of powers between the Executive and the Congress. Parliamentary governments are in a much better position to carry out timely fiscal policy. When the Prime Minister of the United Kingdom and his Chancellor decide upon a fiscal program, either in the annual budget or as an emergency measure, it is as good as enacted. The majority party leadership controls the Parliamentary calendar, and the program will be enacted swiftly if necessary. The President of the United States has no such power, even if his party has majorities in both houses of Congress.

The President submits a budget in January for the fiscal year that begins six months later. But the budget does not emerge from Congress until a year later, and generally is quite different from the one the President proposed. Congressional consideration is fragmented. Appropriations go through many separate committees, and no one is responsible for the total. Tax legislation

76

is independently processed, with only loose relationship to the expenditure budget.

We certainly do need new procedures. It would be desirable to have a Joint Committee on the Budget, which would receive the President's budget message and, with the help of public hearings, appraise and perhaps modify the President's overall recommendations for the size of the budget and the full employment surplus or deficit. The Congress could early in its session vote a resolution on these matters for the guidance of the individual committees dealing with appropriations and taxes. Specific appropriations should leave the President a certain percentage discretion up and down, so that the overall target budget voted can be approximated in practice.[2]

In any case, responsive and flexible fiscal policy requires a mechanism for making prompt, timely, and temporary changes in taxes. In my review of the last decade in previous lectures, I noted the obvious examples of the long delays in our system. The tax cut proposed to Congress in January 1963 was passed in February 1964, to take effect at the beginning of that year. The tax surcharge

---

[2] This issue has come to the fore in the year since the lecture was given. The Congress is beginning to consider new budget procedures. The President has, so far successfully, asserted his right to "impound" appropriated funds he does not wish to spend. Although this brings the budget under control, indeed under tight Executive control, it seems to me constitutionally very dangerous. Congress should have the right to force the Executive to carry out programs it has enacted, unless of course there is a successful Presidential veto. The suggestion in the text would safeguard this right.

first proposed in January 1967 was passed June 28, 1968. These are underestimates of the total lag attributable to our political system. With the powers of a Prime Minister, President Johnson almost surely would have recommended, and his Congressional party would have passed, a tax increase early in 1966, two and a half years before one finally took effect. With somewhat less certainty we can guess that President Kennedy would have accomplished a tax cut in the summer of 1962, one and a half years before the Revenue Act of 1964 became effective.

Both Presidents Kennedy and Johnson proposed machinery for prompt temporary tax changes for purposes of economic stabilization. The Kennedy proposal of January 1962 envisaged a delegation of initiative to the President, subject to Congressional veto. Under the proposal the President could reduce personal income tax rates by as much as five percentage points for a period of six months, unless Congress vetoed his action within thirty days. President Johnson's proposal in 1965 recognized the reluctance of Congress, on political and Constitutional grounds, to delegate tax-making authority to the President. Therefore he invited Congress to consider alternative procedures, free of the taint of delegation. In his last economic message in 1969, President Johnson stressed once again the need for some procedure, whether involving delegation or not, to meet the need. This time, understandably, he spoke of tax increases as well as cuts.

The alternative to delegation is streamlining of procedures in Congress for giving Presidential proposals for temporary tax changes priority in the relevant Congressional committees and on the floors of the House and

Senate. Under either procedure, delegation to the President or Congressional streamlining, advance agreement would be needed on the form of a stabilization tax measure. With this agreement Congressional committees and Congress at large would limit themselves to debating whether the President's proposal is justified by the economic situation. They would not consider all over again whether the appropriate vehicle is income taxation or excise taxation, corporate taxes or personal taxes, tax credits or exemptions or rates, surcharges or discounts proportional to normal tax liability or to tax base. All these issues would have been previously debated and decided, and embodied in the basic legislation setting up the procedure.

The idea is to divorce structural tax legislation from stabilization tax legislation. All the considerations of equity and reform that naturally enter and prolong Congressional debate on tax structure would be excluded from stabilization proposals. Keeping the compartments insulated would take a lot of self-restraint in Congress, or at least a lot of restraint by the committee chairmen and the party leaders. Since one Congress cannot really bind its successor, the procedure might have to be periodically reconfirmed.

Unfortunately, Congress has shown absolutely no interest in proposals of this kind, and because of their sensitive nature no President has spent any political muscle on their behalf. All we can do is keep trying. It would be helpful if the Nixon Administration made this a bipartisan cause.

What tax changes should be the vehicle of flexible

fiscal policy? That is a question where economists can feel more at home. I have already argued, in the first chapter, that temporary tax changes are generally to be preferred to changes of indefinite term. The basic level of federal taxes should be set with a view to the probable and planned trend of federal expenditures, to yield a target full employment surplus or deficit. The appropriate target is not necessarily zero. That depends on the expected and desired balance of private investment and saving at full employment, which in turn depends on the general level of interest rates engineered by the monetary authorities. Both growth considerations and international constraints are involved in deciding the appropriate mix of full employment fiscal and monetary policies. As I argued in the first chapter, a long-run budget policy should not be the accident of short-run crises of stabilization policy, as it will be if permanent tax legislation is altered whenever the economy needs fiscal stimulus or restraint.

In the Presidential proposals for fiscal flexibility the chosen instrument was temporary change in personal income taxes. There is good reason to reconsider this choice. In the second chapter I referred to the distinct possibility that much of the impact of the 1968 surcharge was diluted by taxpayers' awareness that it was temporary. A household free of liquidity constraints could spread the temporary decline in disposable income over its entire consumption horizon. Whether or not this was the main reason for the 1968 disappointment, it seems likely to limit the effectiveness of temporary income tax changes in future, especially if the device is frequently used. It is not safe to operate fiscal policy on the assumption that American consumers are dependent on cash flow for their spending. If that were true, we could control consumption spending simply by varying withholding rates, without changing annual tax liabilities at all! A preferable vehicle is a tax whose imposition and suspension give incentives to consumers and businessmen to shift the timing of their expenditures, a tax which has, in economists' jargon, not just income effects but intertemporal substitution effects.

The investment tax credit is such a device. If it is known to be temporary, it is a powerful incentive to business to make investments at the time the economy needs them. Likewise, during periods when it is suspended, even though their duration is uncertain, business investors have some incentive to postpone projects until it is restored. Perhaps Congress could be induced to allow the President discretion, subject to specified guidelines and criteria, to turn this tax credit on and off. This might not be regarded as a basic infringement of Constitutional prerogative. After all, the Treasury already exercises a great deal of administrative discretion with respect to tax depreciation rules.

I realize that the use of the tax credit for stabilization purposes would not be welcomed by its beneficiaries. Although the Kennedy economists who proposed it in 1961-62 regarded this potentiality as a distinct advantage, Undersecretary of the Treasury Fowler felt he must assure businessmen that the credit would not be a "yo-yo," in order to disarm their initial, and rather inexplicable, coolness to the whole proposal. His reluctance, after he had become Secretary, to violate this assurance was one factor that delayed the Administration's proposal for suspension of the credit in 1966 until September.

The case for using the investment tax credit in counter-cyclical fiscal policy is strengthened by the disabilities of monetary policy in controlling business investment. Although there is plenty of theoretical and empirical reason to believe that the cost of debt and equity finance does influence plant and equipment expenditures, the evidence is that it does so with considerable lag. Corporate investment budgets have a great deal of inertia. Changes in the levels of interest rates and stock prices will affect new budgets when they are made and produce marginal revisions of current budgets. But, in the main, ongoing budgets, especially ongoing projects, will be executed as planned, regardless of conditions in financial markets. In periods of tight money businesses will scramble for the funds needed to carry out their plans. That is why the immediate impact of monetary tightness is shunted to other investors, principally home-builders. That is why we observe monetary tightness in 1966 and 1969 hitting residential construction at once and business investment the following year.

Monetary policy will be further handicapped in future if, as I shall discuss later, its freedom to maneuver is further diminished as interest rates are increasingly internationalized. For these reasons, a powerful nonmonetary device for influencing business investment is very much needed as a tool of stabilization policy, and the investment tax credit fills the bill. Sweden has had considerable success with a similar device, by which corporations can divert some of their profits tax free into special accounts on which they are allowed to draw with tax at any time but without tax only during designated periods.

For consumption a similar effect could be achieved by varying excises on durable goods. In 1971, for example, there was no stabilization reason to *repeal* the 7% automobile excise tax. Suspending it for eighteen months or two years, or until the President determined that the need for economic stimulus had passed, would have given a more powerful incentive to purchase cars now. The same technique could be applied to other consumer durables. Durable goods excises are preferable to general consumption taxes because, like business investment, purchases of durables can be shifted forward or backward in time in response to price incentives.

Some flexibility can also be introduced into transfer programs. There is a strong case for federal supplements to unemployment compensation, triggered on and off when the overall unemployment rate crosses certain thresholds. Besides helping to stabilize aggregate demand, this device would make a marginal improvement in the Phillips curve. At times when a large amount of unemployment is voluntary search, the incentive that unemployment compensation gives for extending search would be diminished.

Preserving the Flexibility of Monetary Policy

Flexibility in fiscal policy is difficult to achieve, but is it needed? Why not let the Federal Reserve do all the fine-tuning? No legislation is required. The Open Market

Committee meets monthly, more often if necessary, and its decisions take effect right away. The trouble is that there are both domestic and international limits on flexible monetary policy.

Domestically, the use of monetary policy encounters resistance because of its uneven impact. I have previously mentioned the heavy share of the burden of monetary restriction absorbed by residential construction. In some degree this allocation is natural and efficient. Houses are very durable. The stock is large relative to the annual flow. When national saving becomes scarce, it is not surprising that highly durable postponable projects are rationed out of contention by rising interest rates. But, so far as housing is concerned, United States financial institutions unnaturally exaggerate this effect. Residential construction is even more vulnerable to tight money than other long-lived postponable projects.

The reason is the dependence of home-building on the flow of savings into specialized mortgage lending institutions, savings and loan associations and mutual savings banks, and into savings and time deposits in commercial banks. These flows are sensitive to market interest rates. The rates offered to savings depositors by these institutions are regulated and sticky; they become less attractive than open market investments in tight money periods and more attractive when market rates are low. This institutional arrangement could be reformed in a number of ways, which it is not necessary to elaborate here. The point of all of them is to let mortgage borrowers have a fair shot at bidding for available saving.

The most important barrier to flexible monetary policy is the ever-increasing international mobility of liquid capital. The Eurodollar market is unifying the short-term money markets of the major countries on both sides of the Atlantic. European countries have felt keenly, and complained bitterly, that they have lost autonomy in monetary policy. Even the autonomy of the United States Federal Reserve has diminished. During recent tight money periods, notably 1966 and 1969, inflows of short-term funds have retarded the rise in our interest rates, and banks have augmented their lendable funds by borrowing in the Eurodollar market. During periods of easy money in the United States, like the winter of 1971-72, we have experienced large outflows of short-term capital. European countries complain in both circumstances. Tight money in the U.S. forces tight money on them, and easy money in the U.S. floods their central banks with unwanted dollars. The interest sensitivity of short-term funds can be expected to continue to increase and to pose even greater problems for the international monetary system and for national monetary policies.

There is no more important item on the agenda of the coming negotiations for international monetary reform. On the one hand, some agreed central coordination of national monetary policies is essential. Otherwise the common international interest rate levels, from which feasible national deviations are limited, will be left to anarchy and tug-of-war. On the other hand, there is nowhere near enough economic and political unity among Europe, North America, and Japan to support a single international monetary policy for the whole group. The new international arrangements must protect some national autonomy in monetary policy.

Recent evolution has been toward essentially uniform

interest rates on short-term open market paper. With finite substitution elasticities, we could hope for differentials sustained long enough to allow deviant national monetary policies to do their domestic work. The resulting international flows of reserves would be very large, and central bankers would have to think much, much bigger than in the past about the size of reserve losses and gains that they accommodate among themselves without sounding the crisis alarm. Even this arrangement could not work unless average or trend interest rate levels were internationally uniform, so that large short-term flows in one direction were reversed by reflows later. And in the limit, as substitution elasticities increase, it cannot work at all; the boundless resources of private arbitrageurs will just erase any rate differentials the national monetary authorities try to create and sustain.

When our own regional Federal Reserve System was established, there was some idea that the separate districts might pursue policies differentiated to their peculiar economic conditions. National unification of money and securities markets made regional diversity of policy impossible. The same could happen internationally. Within the United States the inability of district Federal Reserve Banks to conduct independent policies did not leave the country as a whole in monetary anarchy. The Board of Governors and the Open Market Committee were central authorities. On the contemporary international scene there is no central authority to make policy over the area of unified securities markets. We are faced with the necessity that national money markets must stay in line, but with no mechanism for determining what the line is.

At present the common level of short-term interest rates is the outcome of a kind of international tug-of-war. Because of the size of the United States, the Federal Reserve has the predominant influence. But the Fed is limited by the tolerance of other central banks and governments for dollar holdings. Formerly their threat was to offer dollars for conversion; currently their threat is one way or another to kick over the traces of the whole international monetary and trading system. Unless the rest of the world acquiesces permanently in the fixed-exchange-rate dollar standard to which they seem to have agreed in a fit of absent-mindedness at the Smithsonian meetings of December 1971—an outcome that seems highly doubtful, however much we in this country might like it—we cannot count on a system in which the Federal Reserve makes world monetary policy.[3] Moreover, the Common Market countries will undoubtedly seek greater monetary coordination among themselves, so that Europe will have more muscle in contest with the Federal Reserve. Some agreed arrangements for international coordination are essential.

At the same time it is clearly desirable to preserve some possibilities of autonomy in national or continental monetary policies and to defend them against the grow-

[3] The Smithsonian agreement is now dead. Central bankers were, as it turned out, incapable of thinking "much bigger than in the past about the size of reserve losses and gains that they accommodate among themselves without sounding the crisis alarm." The fixed rate system foundered on huge private flows between currencies, motivated by speculation on changes in rates. Even in the floating rate system which has replaced it, the problem of national autonomy of policy remains.

87

ing internationalization of money markets. Our economies and governments are not sufficiently unified in other respects—goods, labor, and capital markets, taxes and fiscal policies—to live with a single area-wide monetary policy. That is where the analogy with the centralization of Federal Reserve policy breaks down. The same forces that unified short-term securities markets throughout the U.S. also produced more or less national markets in goods, labor, and capital. Interregional movements in these markets can handle regional differences in economic circumstances in a way that is not possible in today's international economy. And a national government can carry out compensatory fiscal redistributions between regions; there is no comparable international mechanism in prospect.

How can some national monetary autonomy be preserved? Some sand has to be thrown into the well-greased channels of the Eurodollar market.

One way is to increase the risk of foreign exchange loss. That is part of the case for greater flexibility of exchange rates, accomplished by outright floating or, within a regime of declared parities, by widened intervention bands and by frequent parity adjustments, whether automatic or discretionary. A wider band adds to exchange risk: possible exchange loss on a three-month bill is significantly greater with a 4% band than with a 1½% band. Exchange risk is also increased if it becomes generally understood that parity changes will be more frequent in future, that they will bear more of the burdens of payments adjustment and other measures correspondingly less.

Exchange flexibility will be a more effective insulating device if parities are kept centered at rates from which movements in both directions are conceivable. If the only way the dollar can go is down, the U.S. will not be able to have lower interest rates than those abroad. This is the advantage of freely floating rates, or of a crawling peg by which the parity is automatically hitched to a moving average of past market rates.

Increasing exchange risk will help, but I do not think we should expect too much from it. Many participants in short-term money markets can afford to take a relaxed view of exchange risk. They can aim for the best interest rate available, taking account of their mean estimate of gain or loss from currency exchange. Multinational corporations, for example, can diversify over time. They will be in exchange markets again and again; there are no currencies that they cannot use.

Stronger measures will be needed to drive a wedge between short-term interest rates in different national markets. One possible measure would be an internationally agreed uniform tax, say 1%, on all spot conversions of one currency into another. This would mean that a three-month Treasury bill in pounds sterling would have to bear an interest rate eight points higher than a dollar Treasury bill before it would be worthwhile for an American who wants dollars in three months to shift. On securities of longer maturity, it would of course take a smaller interest differential to compensate for the exchange tax. But on longer maturities the exchange risk is greater, and the markets are much less perfect anyway.

Under a regime of fixed exchange rates, the interest

rates that international arbitrage tends to equate are nominal rates. That is the source of the paradox that inflation faster than in other countries may improve the balance of payments provided confidence in the established parity is maintained. High nominal interest rates may improve the short-term capital account more than the inflation hurts the trade account. With flexible exchange rates, the interest rates that international arbitrage bring into equality will not be nominal rates but nominal rates plus an allowance for the expected change in the exchange rate. These will be closer to real rates than nominal rates, for the expected trend of exchange rates will normally reflect inter-country differences in expected rates of inflation.

Movement of exchange rates in response to capital flows is a substitute for the movements of international reserves in a regime of fixed exchange rates. Exports and imports respond in turn to the movement of exchange rates. As Mundell has pointed out,[4] the trade balance becomes a component of aggregate demand that government policy can control by measures that raise or lower interest rates relative to those abroad, or by other measures that stimulate capital outflow or inflow and alter exchange rates.

Given the international mobility of funds, exchange flexibility increases the power of monetary policy relative to fiscal policy. In the extreme case of perfect mobility, Mundell showed, monetary policy is powerless with fixed

[4] Robert Mundell, "Capital Mobility and Stabilization Policy Under Fixed and Flexible Exchange Rates," *Canadian Journal of Economics and Political Science*, Nov. 1963, pp. 475-85.

rates, and fiscal policy is powerless with flexible rates. The way expansionary monetary policy works, with flexible exchange rates, is as follows. By lowering domestic interest rates and stimulating capital outflow, the monetary authority causes its currency to depreciate in the exchange market. Exports and import substitutes are stimulated, and domestic income increases until the new money is absorbed in transactions balances at an internationally viable interest rate and stops spilling into foreign exchange markets. The effect of monetary expansion on the export surplus replaces its closed-economy effect on domestic investment, the more so the more complete the international arbitrage of interest rates.

The same mechanism limits the domestic effectiveness of fiscal policy in a world of mobile capital and flexible exchange rates. Expansionary fiscal policy will tend to raise domestic interest rates as it raises income. This will attract funds into the country and cause the currency to appreciate. The adverse effect on the trade balance counters the fiscal expansion. With perfect mobility of capital the offset is complete, and the ultimate outcome is substitution of government spending for foreign investment.

Since monetary policy is the more responsive instrument of domestic stabilization, perhaps we should welcome an exchange rate regime that increases its potency relative to that of fiscal policy. However, when the export-import balance becomes the strategic component of aggregate demand, one country's expansionary stimulus is another country's deflationary shock. We can hardly imagine that the Common Market will passively allow the U.S. to manipulate the dollar exchange rate in the interests of U.S. domestic stabilization. Nor can we imagine the reverse. International coordination of interest-rate policies will be essential in a regime of floating exchange rates, no less than in a fixed-parity regime. Whatever the system, moreover, we need to protect national autonomy in stabilization policy by deliberately contrived obstacles to international flows of funds.

I have one further suggestion to strengthen domestic monetary policy. The monetary authority could operate closer to the margins relevant to the spending decisions it is trying to control. At present the Federal Reserve operates almost wholly in the markets for the shortest and most liquid debt instruments: Federal Funds and Treasury bills. Its direct impact in these markets is transmitted, with the leverage of fractional reserve commercial banking, to other financial markets, eventually effecting the cost and availability of funds for real investment. The linkages of monetary policy to the markets that count—corporate bonds, equities, mortgages, commercial loans—are real enough, but they are often indirect, uncertain, and slow. The short-term markets where the Fed operates are also the most vulnerable to international capital movements.

There are good reasons, of course, why the central bank cannot operate directly in markets for private securities. The proposal, an old one of mine, is that the Treasury issue marketable bonds with purchasing power guarantee.[5] These bonds would be much closer substitutes for physical capital than conventional government securities. Open market operations in the escalated bonds

[5] *Essays in Economics*, Vol. I, Chap. 21.

would give the Fed some control over real rates of interest and increase its influence in markets close to investment decisions. Bonds with purchasing power guarantee have other advantages as well. They would enable insurance companies and pension funds to offer annuities that genuinely protect beneficiaries from risks of inflation.

The Inflation-Unemployment Dilemma[6]

The most ominous challenge to stabilization policy is the incompatibility of our unemployment and inflation goals. Discovery of this hard fact of life has been, as I suggested in the first chapter, the main source of public disillusionment with the New Economics. Squirm as we may, there is really no way out of the impasse. We shall have to face the cruel choice instead of pretending and hoping that it will go away.

A very likely alternative outcome is a policy cycle, as the government's emphasis shifts to the most salient current evil. United States history since the mid-fifties could be interpreted in these terms. Immediately after the inflationary boom of 1955-57, the main emphasis of policy was the conquest of inflationary psychology. After a couple of recessions and three to four years of high unemployment, the Kennedy New Economists set out to restore full employment. Inflation became the main problem again in 1966-69, and the Nixon Administration engineered a recession to overcome inflationary psychology once again. And so it goes.

[6] The points made in this section are elaborated in "Inflation and Unemployment," *American Economic Review*, LXII, March 1972, 1-18.

The "natural rate" theory argues that we do not really have a policy choice. In the long run the trade-off vanishes, the Phillips curve is vertical. We might as well reconcile ourselves, therefore, to the natural rate of unemployment, whatever it is, and orient monetary and fiscal policy wholly to a target rate of inflation. In this view, unemployment should be abandoned as an explicit objective of stabilization policy. I cannot agree, for several reasons.

I agree that we cannot count on sustained money illusion or misperception of wage and price trends to preserve a Phillips trade-off in long-run equilibrium. But I do not agree with the policy conclusion drawn from this observation. The Phillips trade-off is, in my view, essentially a phenomenon of perpetual disequilibrium and adjustment in diverse labor and product markets. In this setting a trade-off lasts long enough for policymakers, if not indefinitely.

The natural rate—an amount of unemployment consistent with zero inflation[7]—has no particular justification on grounds of economic welfare. Given the inflationary bias in mechanisms of wage adjustment, the noninflationary unemployment rate is much larger than could be justified as voluntary or efficient job search activity.

It is not true that a lower unemployment rate cannot

[7] Or, to be precise, with any other steady rate of inflation or deflation. The theory is that when the amount of unemployment is just right, inflation will not continuously accelerate (or decelerate). Price expectations learned from the past will be confirmed by events, whether the expectations are for stability, 10% per year inflation, or 5% a year deflation.

94

be achieved and sustained. What is true, on the natural rate hypothesis, is that it can be achieved and sustained only with accelerating inflation. Acceleration is not necessarily the disaster the word is supposed to connote. In practice it would not occur as inexorably and monotonically as it does in some abstract models of the inflationary process. Anyway, the eventual disutility of accelerating inflation must be weighed against the gains of employment and production in the interim.

Some policies to mitigate the trade-off or lower the natural rate are clearly worthwhile. First, although we do not seem to have had much luck with labor market and manpower policies, we should keep on trying. In particular we need an ambitious program of public service employment, designed to employ and train workers who are not in the mainstream, whose unemployment does very little to discipline the wage increases of workers with more experience, skill, and bargaining power.

Second, although I cannot see legal wage control as a permanent feature of the American scene, I believe there is a case for a loose system of wage guideposts. The emulative wage-wage spiral contains a lot of arbitrariness and indeterminancy. Accordingly, there is an opportunity for devices for mutual de-escalation of wage demands. I gather that this is the function of the construction wage stabilization committee. It can also be the function of a number, say 5½ percent, which acquires some standing as reasonable and legitimate.

Third, one of the sources of inflationary bias is the insensitivity of wage settlements in many labor markets

95

to unemployment and excess supply of labor. Trade unions usually reflect the interests of the employed, not the unemployed or the potential entrants. Perhaps the privileges granted unions under national legislation should be revocable if full membership is not open to all qualified persons, whether unemployed or employed.

Concluding Remarks

THE novelty of the New Economics was exaggerated in the early 1960s, and recent reports of its death are probably exaggerated too. At first the notion that fiscal and monetary policy could keep the economy close to a track of steady growth at full employment encountered deep skepticism and suspicion. But these gave way to high expectations when the economy enjoyed a long period of prosperity and uninterrupted growth, a performance due to a happy conjunction of successful policy and good luck. The euphoria was excessive. Too much was claimed, and even more came to be expected. Some disillusionment was inevitable, especially as the inflationary bias of the economy with sustained full employment became clearer than it was during the recovery of 1961-65.

But the disillusionment was multiplied manyfold by the Vietnam war and deficit financing. Given the massive jolt of 1966, it is hard to imagine any policies that would have kept the economy on even keel or restored stability very quickly. Nonetheless the persistence of inflationary pressure and the disappointing results of several well-advertised policies reenforced skepticism of government's ability to stabilize the growth of the economy and to maintain full employment.

The economic climate after 1966 was favorable to the emergence of an alternative doctrine of government monetary and fiscal policy, and monetarism was ready to occupy the center of the stage. The monetarists blamed erroneous and volatile government measures themselves for economic instability and urged the government to follow a simple and steady course, abandoning its efforts to compensate for swings in private spending. The monetarists also contended that government, under the spell of the New Economics, had relied much too heavily on fiscal policy and that the Federal Reserve, whether influenced by new economics or old, neglected with disastrous consequences the sovereign importance of the quantity of money. For reasons suggested in Chapter 2, I do not believe the monetarist case was ever convincing, either theoretically or empirically. The monetarist tide seems to be waning as experience cumulates to indicate that the world is, to say the least, a lot more complicated than the monetarists' model.

The malaise of the late 1960s and early 1970s touched all aspects of national life, not just the management of the economy. The general discontent fueled some other attacks on economic policy and on the New Economics, more far-reaching and less narrowly professional than monetarism. These attacks challenged the goals of policy rather than the techniques. Until 1965 hardly anyone doubted that economic growth was a very good thing. Subsequently environmentalists, pacifists, anti-materialists, Galbraithians, and neo-Marxists turned it into an unworthy social goal. Before 1965 the fact that economic expansion benefits all segments of society, rich as well as poor, white as well as black, appeared to be a social and

political virtue. Thereafter many critics regarded emphasis on generally shared growth as a cop-out, an excuse for
failure to confront the inequalities and injustices of the
American economy.

In my view, these complaints had some merit. It was
and it is very important to devote more of the resources
of the country to environmental protection and to the
civilian public sector, and equally important to use the
federal fisc to transfer income from the affluent to the
poor. But the attack on the New Economics objectives
of prosperity, full employment, and general economic
growth is misplaced. None of the newer goals of the
critics would have been advanced by consigning the
economy to the stagnation of 1957-60, and none of them
is inconsistent with steady growth at full employment.
Memories are short, and it is all too easy to underrate in
hindsight the seriousness of problems that have been
substantially solved. Stagnation, unemployment, and frequent recession were serious problems before 1961, and
there was good reason to give high priority to their
remedy. *164768*

The task of economic stabilization has proved more
difficult than we thought in those days. In the final chapter I tried to list some lessons of recent experience. Fiscal
policy must be made a sharper and more responsive tool
of macro-economic control. Congress must find a procedure for making a firm overall budget decision, a
procedure in which both economic stabilization and national priorities are considered. On the revenue side, the
country still needs a speedy procedure for adjusting taxes

99

to influence aggregate demand. However, I suggest that the investment tax credit and durable goods excises are better vehicles for such policy than income tax rates.

Even after fiscal reform, monetary measures will remain the major instruments of stabilization policy from month to month and quarter to quarter. Their flexibility must be protected and enhanced: by institutional arrangements which diffuse more widely an impact now concentrated on residential housing, by international monetary devices which preserve some national autonomy in these days where massive liquid funds are poised to move across the exchanges, by providing purchasing-power bonds which the Fed can buy and sell in the open market with greater economic impact than conventional government securities.

With these fiscal and monetary reforms, and with the improved prowess of economic forecasters and econometric model-builders, I believe that the original hope of the New Economics can be fulfilled. That is, active fiscal and monetary policies, dedicated to economic ends and liberated from extraneous taboos, can keep the economy growing within a narrow band of full employment. Not again, I trust, will this hope, along with so many other national aspirations, be betrayed by a Vietnam.

But I cannot end on so optimistic a note with respect to inflation, the economic disease now in the forefront of national attention. Our economy, like all others of the modern world, has an inflationary bias. When it operates without socially intolerable rates of unemployment and excess capacity, prices will drift steadily upward. Maybe they won't gallop as fast as they have in recent years;

100

there were special causes which we hope will not recur. But we are fooling ourselves if we think that chronic inflation can be altogether avoided. There are structural reforms which would mitigate the problem, but they would by no means eliminate it. Moreover, their chances of adoption are poor; they involve very painful surgery on the body politic. I have certainly not done justice to the subject of inflation in this book. As consolation, I can only offer my opinion that inflation is greatly exaggerated as a social evil. Even while prices are rising year after year, the economy is producing more and more of the goods, services, and jobs that meet people's needs. That, after all, is its real purpose.

Index

Library of Congress Cataloging in Publication Data

Tobin, James, 1918-
  The new economics one decade older.

  (Eliot Janeway lectures on historical economics in
honor of Joseph Schumpeter, 1972)
  Includes bibliographical references.
  CONTENTS: Triumph and defeat in the sixties.—
Crossfire from left and right.—Prospects for macro-
economic policy.
    1. United States—Economic policy—1961-
2. Keynesian economics.   I. Title.   II, Series.
HC106.6.T62   338.973   73-16763
ISBN 0-691-04205-5